A JOURNAL TO YOU

SIMI ALEXIS ROMEO

I AM...

Imperfectly Perfect . A Royal . Favoured
Royalty . Valuable . Precious . A Sign
Fearfully Made . Smart . Loved . Blessed
The Salt Of The Earth . Gifted . Resilient
One Of A Kind . An Overcomer . Special
Cherished . At Peace . Lovable . Worthy
Full Of Purpose . Gorgeous . Blessed
Rare . The Daughter Of The Most High
Diadem . Strong . The Light Of The World
Holy . Beautiful . Wonderfully Made
Protected . A Wonder . Distinctive
Fruitful . Chosen . Created In His Image
Imperfectly Perfect . A Royal . Favoured
Royalty . Valuable . Precious . A Sign
Fearfully Made . Smart . Loved . Blessed
The Salt Of The Earth . Gifted . Resilient
One Of A Kind . An Overcomer . Special
Cherished . At Peace . Lovable . Worthy
Full Of Purpose . Gorgeous . Blessed
Rare . The Daughter Of The Most High
Diadem . Strong . The Light Of The World
Holy . Beautiful . Wonderfully Made
Protected . A Wonder . Distinctive
Fruitful . Chosen . Created In His Image
Imperfectly Perfect . A Royal . Favoured
Royalty . Valuable . Precious . A Sign
Fearfully Made . Smart . Loved . Blessed
The Salt Of The Earth . Gifted . Resilient
One Of A Kind . An Overcomer . Special
Cherished . At Peace . Lovable . Worthy

ISBN: 978-1-8381092-2-6

DEDICATION

I am so grateful to the Lord God Almighty for giving me the opportunity to write this novel. Thank you for trusting me.

I would also like to thank my mum, who has always strived to do the best for me and shown me a great amount of love, my dad, who has taught me how to value myself over and over again, and my big brother Seun, who has been a constant source of support, but also laughter in my life. I appreciate you all.

Thank you to the Romeo and Rockson clan! Family is everything, and each of you has impacted me in different ways. Special shout out to uncle Bayo and aunty Kemi! Having lived with you for three years during my teenage years, you gave me the greatest gift - the gift of God.

Thank you to all my many aunties, uncles, and mentors in my life. Whether it's going out of your way to listen to my ideas, or pushing me in my faith, you have done it all, and I am so grateful for the love you have shown me.

My friendships! It took me a while to have such profound and impactful people in my life. But it was definitely worth the wait. You know yourselves, and I thank you for just loving me for who I am and encouraging me. A lot of you were there when I was going through my trying times to find myself, and you still stuck by me even though I wasn't the best person to be around. Thank you for believing in me.

Holding Forth The Word Ministries! This is the church I grew up in, in Milton Keynes. I will forever be grateful to you for shaping me into the woman I am today. The Bible verse, "Train up a child the way he should go, and when he is old, he will not depart from it," Proverbs 22:6 is true. I moved from that church when I was 16, and although I went through struggles in my life, the word of God never departed from me. Thank you.

Jesus House! My current church. I dedicate this book to you,

you started the beloved Esthers Mentoring Scheme (EMS), where I was reminded of my worth, of how strong I am, and that my life has a purpose. This scheme has changed hundreds of lives, and many of the nuggets from there, have been used as the basis of the characters in the story.

And you, 'The Reader'! Thank you so much for supporting this book. My prayer is that you will go on your own personal journey and discover that you are not only valuable and are incredibly strong, but your life has its own specific purpose, and you will fulfil it.

Stay blessed!

Lots of Love,

Simi Alexis Romeo

CHAPTER ONE

Kika

Kika could not take her eyes off her computer screen. She had been gazing at her one-page article over and over again, scrolling up and down the page and meticulously studying every word, sentence, and paragraph. She had been working on this piece for weeks and had researched every possible angle to ensure there were no grammatical errors. She was desperate for it to be nothing other than perfect.

For as long as she could remember, Kika's dream was to be the top journalist in the big city of Lagos, Nigeria, where she grew up - she felt this was part of her purpose. As a child, she would always pretend she was a top reporter and interview her friends and family. When all her friends were watching Disney Channel and Nickelodeon, Kika wanted to watch the news with her father. She loved it and found it captivating.

As she grew older, she had felt that to be a top journalist, she would need to work at the top media company,

'Hello Lagos' the leaders in the industry. During her university days, she had offered herself up for free internships to the point where she built a rapport with the workers there. When she finally graduated, they offered her a position straight away. That was eight years ago, and Kika felt she was still at the bottom of the ladder.

"Wow, Kika? Please do not tell me that this is still the same article on 'Up and Coming Musicians' you have been working on for the past month?" Daisy questioned as she looked over her shoulder and watched Kika going through her article. She was Kika's closest colleague at work. They had both started at 'Hello Lagos' around the same time, but Daisy worked in a different department.

"Unfortunately," Kika sighed. "It is nearly there, just a few more tweaks." She knew Daisy was probably wondering why she had put in such an enormous effort into writing a story that was not of great interest, especially when this was not the first 'unpopular' article she had written. However, Kika felt 'Up and Coming Musicians' would definitely attract some interest from the younger generation. Plus, she was trying to impress her terrifying boss, Ms Gozy, The Editor- in Chief at 'Hello Lagos'. Kika wanted her boss to see her potential and maybe, give her more responsibility like a possible promotion.

Ms Gozy was a strong character who was incredibly hard to please. She had built 'Hello Lagos' from the ground up, into the number one pop culture media company, and is very much respected in the industry. She relies heavily on Kika, but not as a journalist - more as an assistant. Over the past eight years, Kika would be at Ms Gozy's beck and call. From booking her appointments to running errands for her and her children. Meanwhile, when there was a major story to cover at work, Kika would be assigned to it and be made to feel like it was her article and do all the hard work; but at the end of the day, Ms Gozy would take full credit for the piece. As a result, Kika had always been passed up for promotion, and her efforts and contributions were never recognised. Her friends and family would always advise her to quit and go somewhere she would be 'valued', but they could never understand her decision to stay put. "Where else would she get an opportunity like this?" she would say to herself. This company was at the top, going anywhere else would imply going backwards, and Kika was not prepared to do that.

"Daisy, can you please have a read? I really don't want there to be any silly mistakes," Kika said, stepping back from her laptop, allowing Daisy to come closer to go through the article.

Daisy could not stop smiling the whole way through reading it. "Kika, honestly, you are so talented. I do not see how Ms Gozy could make this any better," she said, smiling at her. Although Kika never expressed her concerns to Daisy, she understood how her friend struggled with being recognised.

Kika smiled back, relieved, "oh, thank God!" She printed out the draft and headed to Ms Gozy's office, secretly hoping that all the hard work she had put in would be appreciated, and she would get some recognition.

As she arrived, she said a quick prayer under her breath.

"God, please let this go well according to your will."

"Come in," a stern voice came from behind the door.

Kika slowly turned the door handle and walked into Ms Gozy's office.

"Good afternoon, Ms Gozy," she said.

A gorgeous, poised woman in her signature turban looked up from her desk, "Kika, what can I do for you?"

Kika took a deep breath while nervously handing the

article to her petrifying boss. "I just wanted to show you the article I wrote for the 'Up and Coming Musicians' in Lagos."

Ms Gozy looked at Kika confused, as she took the A4 sheet of paper from her. "I was not aware you were writing this," she said.

Kika paused, "Well, you told me about a month ago that you were thinking of writing an article on it. So I took the initiative, did my research, and put it all together," Kika said anxiously smiling and hoping her boss would appreciate her for stepping up to the plate without being asked.

Ms Gozy read through the article, occasionally nodding her head.

"Kika, this is a fantastic read," she said monotonously after reading through it.

Kika's eyes lit up, "Oh, really? Wow, thank you so much!"

"…but, we cannot run the story," Ms Gozy said, slowly breaking her heart. "I gave this story to someone else a couple of weeks ago. It would be unfair to take it away from them."

"Oh," Kika said dismayed, "well, could we not co-write it?" She continued, trying to hide the fact she was disappointed.

Ms Gozy laughed, "We do not do that here; you should know that."

Kika was disappointed. She had thought about speaking to Ms Gozy about the article beforehand, but she wanted to blow her away. "Well, you think the article is good, right?"

"Yes, I do," She said with a smile.

"Well, that leads me to my main question. I would love

to have more responsibility here, maybe to be trusted with some top stories to write?"

Ms Gozy laughed, "But hunny, you do not have experience."

Kika was irritated. First of all, she found Ms Gozy annoyingly condescending when she called her 'hunny'. Secondly, she had been a loyal employee for eight years and was now really frustrated at Ms Gozy's refusal to allow her acquire the experience that she needed. "But how can I have experience if I am not given any responsibility?"

"Please, do not throw your toys out of the pram; your time will come." Ms Gozy said smugly. "I have put a list together to keep you busy since you have so much time to be doing things I never asked you to do," she said whilst smirking.

Kika looked at the piece of paper she took from Ms Gozy. It was filled with a long list of people to call and multiple appointments to make on her behalf. She struggled not to roll her eyes for fear that her frustration would be sensed. "Okay, thank you," she said as she left her office.

As Kika headed back to her seat completely aggravated, she began to notice how she was feeling. It took her back to a place of disapproval, hurt, and pain. Growing up, Kika was incredibly insecure as she always felt unwanted - last to be picked for anything, and easily forgotten. When she met people for the first time, they initially seemed to adore her and love her for her great and fun personality. However, once they got to know her on a deeper level, they appeared not to be as enthusiastic as they once were. For this reason, Kika grew up feeling disregarded and unappreciated by others. She felt there was something wrong with her.

Kika Taiwo was part of a 'strong' friendship group - her friends included:

Anita Fawun - who was beautiful, rich, smart, and got everything she pretty much wanted. Anita was Kika's best friend from childhood and was probably the closest person to her.

Tara Williams - who could be pretty catty, but had a good heart. She was also very close to Anita, and sometimes Kika felt Tara was always in competition with her to be Anita's best friend. Kika found it hilarious as she thought no one could ever come between her and Anita.

Mimi Coker - who had a heart of gold, but Kika always felt Mimi would choose Tara and Anita over her. If they were all having a disagreement, Kika felt Mimi would always take their side even when they were blatantly in the wrong.

To the outside world, the four best friends were as thick as thieves. They had each other's backs and stood firm. Kika loved being perceived in this way, as good friendships were incredibly important to her. However, inside of her, Kika knew they were not as strong as they came across. She noticed that she would give 110% to each of them while they never managed to meet her expectations of what a true friend should give. Throughout their teenage years, her friends would continuously break her heart and not be as supportive as she would expect. She sometimes felt overlooked, and she struggled with this feeling so much that they had countless arguments about how she did not feel valued enough by them.

It got to a point when she realised that living a life like this was not healthy. It was not healthy for her friends to have her being so defensive, and it was not healthy for her to dwell on these thoughts. She knew that she needed to sort out these personal issues, or she was going to lose her friends for good.

This is how Kika came to grow her relationship with

God. She realised she could not put her trust in human beings as they were bound to fail you, and she could only really rely on God. As she developed a closer relationship with Him, she became more confident in herself, and she became more likeable to her friends and others. She made this discovery five years ago and now feels she has over-come this feeling of insecurity. But when she gets mistreated and dismissed by Ms Gozy, that negative feeling creeps back in.

"How did it go?" Daisy asked anxiously as Kika plonked herself down at her desk.

Kika looked over at Daisy, raising one eyebrow. "Well, she loved the article -"

"That's great!" Daisy said ecstatically.

"...but she isn't going to run it," Kika said, folding her arms.

"Aww, that sucks Kika. I am so sorry to hear that," Daisy said, trying to offer her comfort. "I know! Let's go for a nice meal to get your mind off everything."

Kika liked that idea. "Give me ten minutes. I just need to make a few calls for Ms Gozy, and I am all yours."

"Kika, there's a guy who would not stop looking at you," Daisy said excitedly, sitting opposite Kika at a local restaurant.

Kika looked behind her to see this tall, dark-skinned man with a nice beard looking over at her.

"Oh, he is handsome," she said while turning back to Daisy.

Kika was fed up with the single life and desired to meet the right person. She was 28 and was not getting any younger, as her mother and father both liked to remind her constantly. For all her friends, it was so easy for them to find someone, but for her, not so much. She knew what she wanted, but she was not even meeting the kind of guys that she felt were 'husband material'. She would meet all these 'dodgy' guys who were not serious or would lie that they were single, whilst in actual fact, they were engaged or even married. Or she would get involved with a guy who made it seem like he had the right intentions, but she would invariably end up in a year-long 'situationship' - a relationship that remains undefined. People would often say - 'it is where you are going' or 'it is who you are hanging out with.' Kika was very wary of people's opinions on why she was single; she knew it had nothing to do with where she was going or who she hung out with. It just happened to be the plan God had for her.

"Ring check?" she said to Daisy.

Daisy subtly looked over at the man and looked at his finger. "No ring," she said, smiling.

Kika turned around and purposely caught his eye and smiled, which made him feel comfortable enough to come over to talk to her.

The girls looked at each other and quietly shrieked as this tall, handsome man came towards them.

"Hi, I'm Femi, you ladies are looking beautiful."

"Hi, Femi, thank you. I am Kika, and this is Daisy," Kika said with a smile.

"Hi," Daisy said, blushing.

"I don't mean to sound too forward when I say this, but you have the most beautiful skin I have ever seen," Femi said to Kika, admiring how smooth her milk-chocolate coloured skin looked.

Kika blushed, as she tucked her long black weave behind her ears, "Why, thank you - shea butter." She said cheekily.

"Would you ladies like to join us at our table?" he asked, not taking his eyes off Kika's big brown eyes.

"Thank you for asking, but we are having a girls' night tonight. Hope you can understand?"

Daisy gave Kika a strange look.

"I understand," he said, smiling, "well, may I have your number?" Femi asked.

Kika nodded and typed her number into Femi's phone.

"What was that about?" Daisy asked Kika as soon as Femi left their table.

"Ever heard about playing hard to get," Kika said smugly, "we cannot just drop our nice girlie night out for a man."

Daisy rolled her eyes. "Whatever, let's get the bill."

When the waiter came over, he let the girls know their food had already been paid for by Femi.

Daisy laughed, "wow, what a keeper!"

Kika was irritated, "where is he?" She said to the waiter.

"He has left," the waiter responded.

Kika was not a fan of a man feeling like she could be bought - she found it controlling. "Now we owe him something," She said to Daisy.

"You are reading too much into it, girl. He was just being a gentleman".

Kika shook her head - Daisy had no idea.

That evening, Kika had just finished taking a shower and slowly got into bed. She reached across to her bedside table drawer and brought out her journal. Journaling was something Kika had been doing every single night for years, and it was like therapy to her. It was a time she felt she could really express herself, and about how events in the day had made her feel. She also found it incredibly encouraging to look back at past days and remind herself of the good times she had experienced.

Kika journaled about how Ms Gozy made her feel about the article, how it took her to a place in the past that she hated. She wrote about going for drinks and meeting Femi and how, although she did not like the fact he had paid for her and Daisy's dinner, she was still excited to have met him. Just as she put her journal down and tucked herself into bed, her phone vibrated, and a notification popped up on her screen.

[Hi Kika, this is Femi from earlier on. How are you?]

Kika smiled. She opened the message and began to respond.

Anita

"Nati…I'm pregnant!" Anita ran to her husband with a positive pregnancy test. She gazed into his eyes, eager to experience the reaction she had dreamt of for years—that pleasant reaction of pure joy that would signal that their delay had finally come to an end. Nati and Anita had been happily married for seven years and had longed for a child throughout their union. Medical professionals had consistently assured the couple that there were no issues and therefore, no medical reason for their infertility. This ironically only made the couple more anxious and nervous about whether or not their desire to be parents will ever become a reality.

They had gone through numerous fertility treatments and even participated in In-Vitro Fertilisation (IVF) therapies, but all were unfortunately unsuccessful. They had also briefly looked into adoption, but Nati was strongly against this. He wanted his very own child, his blood, whereas Anita was more than happy just being a parent to any child. However, due to Nati's disinterest in the adoption option, she was forced to drop the idea and had concluded that having children and being a mother was just not part of her purpose.

Now it seemed that there was hope for the couple to have children naturally and that their wait had finally come to an end. The end of awkward family functions where distant relatives believe they have the right to question their lack of children and proceed to make insensitive comments about how 'time is running out' and how Anita's 'biological clock is ticking'. Some relatives even dared to shame them for 'deliberately and willingly' stopping the procession of future generations.

Nati and Anita always kept their fertility problem hidden away from their family. They felt it was critical to protect each other and not have others judge them, fabricating reasons for why this is so. Anita was made to feel ashamed by others for being a married woman without children because in the Nigerian culture, not being able to have children is seen as a curse. So, Nati and Anita were united in giving the same response to every question thrown their way - "It is just not what we are thinking about right now," and they remained steadfast in this response.

Nati leaped towards his wife, "are you serious?" He yelled while wrapping her in his arms. He looked into her eyes and gently held her face in the palm of his hands and whispered. "No, seriously, are you serious?"

They both fell to the sofa, elated and full of so much joy. This was really happening, and they honestly couldn't believe that God had finally answered their prayers.

Anita Fawun had always been the girl that got everything she ever wanted. She grew up in Lagos, Nigeria, with her parents and two younger sisters - Ari and Jade. She was incredibly smart and got into the top schools of her generation - both in Nigeria and the United Kingdom, where she went to further her education. Her family are exceedingly wealthy - her late father, Tayo Fawun, owned Fawun Investment Limited - the top investment banking company in Africa. He worked extremely hard, and Anita always playfully called him the 'Bank of the Fawuns'. Her father was never available emotionally as he was always away working, but Tayo loved his family exceptionally and did everything for them financially. Anita's mother - Aisha Fawun, was a lady of leisure. She was titled "the MD of the Fawun Household" by her daughters - it was like running a business. She managed the chef, the drivers, the cleaners, the nannies, the children, and her most demanding 'employee', her husband. She was always well put together, and their home was immaculate. Anita always saw her mother as her role model and desired to live a life just like hers. She intended to marry a wealthy man and only be responsible for taking care of their household. She was practically there; she was just missing the 'children' part.

Anita met Nati during her time at University College London (UCL) - she was in her second year studying Law and Finance, while he was doing a Masters' course in Business. They met in the University Library. Nati was there looking to meet up with his course-mates for a study session when he saw Anita sitting by herself doing independent studying. She had an aura of elegance and grace about her. She had beautiful glowing caramel skin with natural soft textured hair, which she had neatly put into a bun. She sat at the desk with a great posture and was focused. He was intimidated by her beauty, which made him decide to walk away and continue searching for his course-mates. When he eventually settled down to study, he could hardly concentrate because Anita was all he could think about. As soon as the study session ended, he went back to where she had been seated, but she was nowhere to be seen. Nati was unable to forget her and was desperate to see her again. In the next few weeks, he consistently searched for the mysterious girl from the library. He made a point to go to the library every day, hoping to stumble upon her again. He religiously described her to friends and searched for her on social media, but it seemed as if looking for Anita was like looking for a needle in a haystack.

A month had passed, and Nati was beginning to lose hope of ever finding Anita. There was a charity fashion show event being run by the African Caribbean Society (ACS) at their University, which Nati and his friends had planned to attend. At the event, he sat down with his friends towards the back to watch the show. One of the fashion designers - Tara Williams, blew the crowd away with her designs. Her models were gorgeous, and one in particular caught Nati's eyes - it was the girl he had been looking for. She walked down the runway, smiling, 'selling' the clothes. "That's her," he tapped his friend's shoulder. And now that he had found her, he was determined not to lose her again.

As soon as the show ended, Nati hurried backstage in the hope of finding Anita. He waited outside the door for a few minutes when he eventually saw Tara and Anita leaving.

"Hey, Tara Williams - your line was amazing," he nervously said.

Tara looked at this gorgeous man in front of her, "oh, why, thank you," she smiled, "what's your name?"

"I am Osinachi Edoh - but everyone calls me Nati." He looked over at Anita, who was smiling at him. "And you looked gorgeous on the runway - really selling your friend's line - what is your name?" He said, putting out his hand.

Anita looked up at Nati. He was about 6"2, he had gorgeous chocolate skin, and his body was built like an athlete's. This guy was more than fine and definitely Anita's type.

"Hi, I'm Anita Fawun, nice to meet you, Nati," she reciprocated the handshake.

"Well to celebrate this night, a group of friends and I are going to a bar later, would you girls like to come?" Nati kindly asked, trying not to come across as too forward.

They both smiled and nodded excitedly. Nati brought out his phone to exchange numbers with them.

From that day on, Nati and Anita dated for three solid years at the end of which Nati popped the question during a family holiday in Dubai. They got married, and the wedding was the talk of the town. Every media house, celebrity, and public personality wanted to be at the Fawun-Edoh 'wedding of the year'. Social media was agog for #anatilove.

As soon as they were married, Anita's parents bought them a four-bedroom townhouse in Ikoyi – one of the most prestigious neighbourhoods in Lagos, along with two SUV motor vehicles. Although Nati had also been doing quite well, when they got married, Anita's father offered him a stake in his company, along with a full-time role as an investment banker. Her father loved him so much that when he passed away two years ago, his "son" had been positioned to become the Chief Financial Officer (CFO) of Fawun Investment Limited.

Life was good to Anita and Nati, and six months into their marriage, they decided to start trying for a baby. But somehow, six months turned into seven years. After multiple doctors' appointments and twenty-seven failed pregnancy tests, Anita finally got the positive sign which she was now so happy to be sharing with her husband.

"Babe, we need to call your mother, she needs to be the first to know," Anita said excitedly. She had always had a very awkward relationship with her mother-in-law. She always felt she had an underlining passive aggressiveness towards her, and Anita never understood why. The fact that Anita had not given her a grandchild only made their relationship more strained.

Nati's mother, Gloria, was a humble woman who raised him as a single mother. She struggled financially for years and felt Anita, on the other hand, had grown up with a silver spoon in her mouth. Therefore, she was not the right person for her son - even after being with each other now for over ten years. She was not keen on the Fawun family. "They are too wealthy, they can't fear God," She would tell her son. "Anita is a spoilt child who is going to kill you, my son, with her spoilt ways."

Nati, on his part, would always make excuses for his mother's offensive opinions and did not acknowledge Anita's discomfort.

"Mum! Mum!" Nati screamed down the telephone.

"Osinachi, why are you shouting this early in the morning?" Gloria said, half asleep.

"I'm sorry, mum, but we cannot wait to tell you - I am with Anita right now, we have some exciting news."

Gloria rolled her eyes and sighed at the sound of Anita's name, "please surprise me, dear."

Anita felt the uncomfortable tension and awkwardly screamed, "mum, I'm having a baby - we have just found out," she clenched her fists into her husband's hands very tightly. She felt so anxious, hoping that today will be the start of a newfound closeness between her and her mother-in-law.

Gloria was speechless. She had given up on the idea that she would ever be a grandmother and had self-labelled Anita as being less than a woman.

"Mum are you there?" asked Nati.

"When Jesus says yes, nobody can say no," Nati's mother started singing down the telephone. Tears had begun to flow down her face. She was ecstatic. "Ah, ah! Praise God! I am going to be a grandmother - God is good!" She screamed.

Nati and Anita started laughing and dancing to Gloria's singing. At that moment, there was no tension, no discomfort, and no pain. Everybody was overwhelmed with joy and happiness. Their life was about to change, and they couldn't wait.

Tara

"I was thinking baby blue and silver for my traditional wedding colours," Tara said to Mimi, her wedding planner and one of her best friends. Tara was excited to finally be getting into planning her wedding, which she had waited so many years for. Bode Cole, her husband-to-be, was a renowned businessman in Nigeria. He was the love of Tara's life and ticked all her boxes in what she wanted in a man. She could not wait to be Mrs Tara Cole.

"The colours are gorgeous, Tara," Mimi said while writing down the confirmed choices in her wedding planning journal. "So, have you thought about whether or not you are inviting your mother yet?" Mimi asked Tara, trying not to beat around the bush.

Tara was unsure; she had a tumultuous relationship with her mother, who blamed her for one of the most painful experiences of her life. Tara's mother, Tola Williams, was unfortunately raped by her math tutor at the age of sixteen. He did not only rape her, he was also the man who took her virginity. Consequently, she became pregnant with Tara. Although she tried to love the child, it was evident that she saw her as the pain that she had experienced. Tola wanted desperately to abort the pregnancy, but Tara's grandmother convinced her that although the situation was not ideal, there had to be a reason that God allowed her to become pregnant with a child in the first place. She encouraged her to have the baby and promised that she would raise the child.

Unfortunately, Tara's grandmother passed away unexpectedly when Tara was just seven. Tola was still adamant about not raising Tara herself and sought to give her up for adoption. But her sister, Tara's aunty Lola, chose to take over the responsibility of caring for Tara. This meant that all of a sudden, Tara had to move to the United Kingdom to live with her aunty who had a daughter of a similar age to her, Dabira. Dabira and Tara consequently grew up together and pretty much became sisters.

Tara felt her mother's absent love for her deeply. As a young girl, her grandmother and aunty did their best to hide her mother's rejection of her, but Tara always knew deep down there was an issue. They would be at family functions, and Tara's mother would avoid her like the plague.

When she turned sixteen, she sat her aunty down and asked her to explain why her mother was never in the picture; and even when they did see each other, why she never tried to spend any time with her?

"Tara, I think you are now old enough to know the true story," Aunty Lola said. At this point, she knew she could not hold back as Tara was at an age where she felt it was time to explain the mystery. This was how Tara found out the whole truth about her birth and the reasons for her mum's rejection.

Although it was comforting to Tara that somebody still wanted her, it was extremely hurtful that the one person in the world who is supposed to love her unconditionally sees her as a reminder of their pain. This had a profound effect on Tara's psyche. It gave her a deep sense of insecurity and made her feel like she was never good enough. She grew up always comparing herself unfavourably to others. She compared the love her aunty had for her against what she felt she had for her cousin Dabira, her own child. She compared herself to her friends and people in her class. She compared herself to people in her age group that she did not even know. This insecurity influenced her relationships - in her friendship group, Tara was always on the defensive, the effects of the significant abandonment issues she suffered from.

After she graduated from University, Tara moved back to Nigeria for her national youth service (NYSC), a scheme graduates are expected to go through in order to be able to work in Nigeria. During that time, she met Bode, fell in love, and when her national service year came to an end, she chose to stay in Nigeria with him.

"I guess I will invite her," Tara said, eventually answering Mimi's question. "I just feel aunty Lola should be more celebrated that day as she raised me, after all." Mimi wrote this down in her journal.

"Hello Mimi, how are you?" Bode said while coming into the living room where the ladies were having their meeting.

Tara immediately stood up to stand next to her husband to be, "Hey babe! We were just finalising the guestlist for the wedding. Mimi has everything under control."

"How many people do we have at the moment for the church wedding?" Bode asked.

"We have about 950 people," Mimi said.

"What!" Bode looked incredulously at Tara, "We agreed we were inviting 500 people maximum!" 500 people was still quite tricky for Bode. He was not a fan of large Nigerian events. If he had it his way, he would have a wedding abroad with a guest list of 85.

"I know we agreed on 500 people, but I was thinking about the so many other people I know; it would be cruel not to invite them."

"I understand this, but our wedding is not a concert, Tara, we have to feed all these people. How can we afford food for 950 people?"

"Look, guys, I am going to leave you to discuss this," Mimi said, tactfully getting her things together. "Tara, please let me know your decision on this," she whispered as she left their 3-bedroom apartment in Lekki.

Tara was irritated by Bode's comment. What did he mean by "how can we afford it?" They were rich as far as she was concerned. She was embarrassed that Bode had said that in front of Mimi.

Bode could sense Tara's frustration as she stared at him with her almond-shaped cat eyes while raising her strong thick eyebrows. He loved Tara's face, but not when she was this angry. He, however, was adamant that she was being irrational.

"Thanks a lot, Bode. Now Mimi is going to tell people we cannot afford to feed people," Tara said, folding her arms and throwing herself back onto the couch.

"Tara, you are not being reasonable. We agreed 500

people - 950 will blow our budget," Bode tried to explain logically.

"Bode, Mimi told me that when Anita and Nati got married, they had 900 guests."

"And what does that have to do with us and our relationship?" Bode asked, confused.

"Well, if we have 950, this will mean our wedding will be a lot more popular than theirs," Tara explained, confident that she had a case.

"Tara, why does this matter? We are not Anita and Nati," Bode said frazzled.

"Exactly, we are better. We have more people attending, and we will also have like a premarital beach party, premarital dinner, premarital award show - Mimi and I have come up with so many ideas," Tara said excitedly.

"Award show?" Bode was angry. Tara was so concerned about being better than her peers, she had no concern about their relationship and financial situation. "Tara, you really need to get your priorities straight. We have a budget of N40 million for both the Yoruba Traditional and White weddings, and that budget includes our honeymoon. If you want to use it to pay for 950 people you could care less about, that is on you. I am fine either way." Bode stood up and left the living room to cool off in the kitchen, hoping Tara will eventually come to her senses.

Tara stayed seated, thinking about the budget. The last quotation Mimi had given her had come to a total of N35 million for both weddings. However, this did not include the additional premarital events she desired to have. She could see where Bode was coming from, but he did not understand how stressful it was, being the ugly duckling and the poor friend in the group. This was what Tara thought of herself, not necessarily how others viewed her.

One of the reasons she felt like this was because she compared herself to others a great deal - especially to Anita. Anita always outdid her in every possible way. When they were in school, Anita would always get better grades. When they would go on nights out, all the guys would always want to get to know Anita, and Anita was also the first to get married in their friendship group, and people still talk about her wedding seven years on. For her sake, Tara knew she needed to top that wedding.

She got up swiftly to try and catch up with Bode.

"Wait, Bode," Tara exclaimed.

Bode heard Tara calling after him and was happy as it seemed as though Tara had finally come to her senses.

"Bode, I have an idea, and I am willing to compromise."

Bode turned around and smiled, "oh yeah?"

"We can sell Aso-Ebi for people to wear to the wedding for N100,000 apiece. If it is the wedding of the year, people will want to attend and will be prepared to pay that much to be a part of it."

Bode sighed. Aso-Ebi is a uniformed fabric that is traditionally worn at Nigerian social events to show solidarity with the celebrants. These days, however, people tend to add to the price to make money off their guests.

"And then if just about half of the 950 people attending the wedding buy it, we can make about N40 million profit, just on fabric sales alone", Tara continued, impressed by her quick math and genius idea.

"Tara, is our marriage a business to you? You really need to think and get your priorities right. We are not getting married to be the wedding of the year. We are getting married because we love one another and want to spend the rest of our lives together. Is that not what you want?"

"Of course, it is what I want Bode, but can we not just have both?" Tara said, trying to reason with him.

"We could have both if we could afford it, but I am quite disappointed that you feel that scamming your close friends is the way to go about it." Bode sat down to put his shoes on.

"Where are you going?" Tara asked confused.

"I am going to the golf club to chill with my guys, and I am going to pray that when I get back, you would have gotten your priorities straightened out," Bode said, walking out.

Tara watched as Bode left their home, she was sad that she disappointed him, but she still felt Bode did not understand her side of things. He did not know what it was like to always be the odd one out and oppressed by her friends. Having this big wedding will make her happy. Why did Bode not care about making her happy?

A journal to the reader

Dear Reader,

Insecurity is such a massive part of most people's lives. I have noticed that it is a lot more common than one would think.

From the first chapter, you can see how all three characters have shown signs of insecurity in different ways, but it all stems from other people's perceptions of them. Kika has grown up feeling insecure because of how her friends saw her. Anita felt insecure because of her situation of not being able to have children for so long and how her mother-in-law never cared to know her. Tara felt insecure because she grew up with her mother abandoning her.

This brings me to this fundamental question, who determines your value?

I remember when people would label me and tell me what I am.

"Simi, your voice is so high-pitched, and you sound like a baby."

"Simi, you are so short."

"Simi, you are so loud."

These were all meant to be said in jest and as jokes. But when you think about the context of what they are saying, I mean it is true. I do have a childlike nature, I am only 5ft 2, and I am a generally a loud person. But the way people were telling me this was not in an appreciative way. Oh no, they were faulting me. It happened so much, I began to fault myself. They were putting me down for things which honestly, I could not change.

These statements came from people I was around a lot. They probably did not realise how much of an impact it could have on me, but It did.

I would always feel my height was setting me back, or the fact that I look young and sound young means I would not be taken seriously. I even remember one of my friends in primary *school told me if I continue speaking the way I do, nobody will take me seriously.*

I'd do everything possible to change myself to ensure I become who they expect me to be- but it did not work. I am about to be 27 still sound like I am about five, I am still short, and I am still loud naturally.

Have I been taken seriously? Actually, there are times people have not taken me seriously, but guess what I discovered?

They miss out when they dismiss me. Why? - because I determine my value. I know how great God made me. I know those that really know me, love me for who I am, and, most importantly, I know what God says about me.

He says I am Valuable.

The Bible says that he "created me in his own image" - Genesis1:27

The Bible says "He knitted me together in my mother's womb" - Psalm 139:13

The Bible says that "I am fearfully and wonderfully made" - Psalm 139: 14

These scriptures focus not only on my appearance but also on my personality, my experiences, and my emotions.

So why would I take another imperfect person's advice? Especially when they are probably going through their fair share of problems and struggles themselves.

So, what about you?

Are there labels people have put on you that still affect you today?

Are there situations where people have dismissed you and have not seen the value in you?

Bear in mind these people could be your enemies, but they could also be those closest to you - classmates, friends, and even family. Remember what God says about you. Remember how special you are.

Sometimes other people and experiences could make you act and react in a certain way that you are not proud of, but it is okay. Nobody is perfect. God has given us the gift of transformation. The important thing is that you recognise that you are not perfect, and you are willing to change.

Journal Task 1: Write down labels that people have used for you all over a page. Once you have finished, cross them out. This is a sign that your value has nothing to do with what others say about you. Especially others that don't really value you and know the real you. As you cross them out, say this scripture:

In my eyes, you are a brand new creation. The old has passed away, the new has come" - 2 Corinthians 5:17

Tip: Guard your heart against those that don't have your best interest at heart. Not everyone is going to appreciate what God has put into you, but the important people will. Remember that!

Lots of Love X

Simi Alexis Romeo

CHAPTER TWO

Anita

"I'll have some avocado on toast, please," Kika said to the waiter.

Sunday afternoons were usually dedicated to Anita's weekly brunch date with her best friends, Kika, Mimi, and Tara. They had all been friends since secondary school and had grown into adulthood together. Anita was aware that they were all at different stages of life and had so much going on that it was essential to intentionally make an effort to catch up regularly to socialise and update each other on the goings-on in their lives.

During these times, Anita always felt there was nothing particularly exciting about her life - she had always been married to Nati - and therefore usually had nothing new to add to the conversation. However, she loved hearing about Kika's dating life and all the so-called 'demons' out there; Tara was in the middle of planning her wedding, and Mimi was running her event planning business while raising her two children. Nonetheless, today was different;

she could not wait to tell the girls about her 'bun in the oven'.

"So what's this exciting news! I can't wait," asked Mimi.

Anita looked at her friends, "girls, I'm so excited to tell you that Nati and I - ," she paused.

"Yes…," they all said eagerly.

"Nati and I are expecting a baby!" She screamed.

They all repeated the scream. They knew how much this situation had affected Anita. It had gotten to a point where she had stopped speaking about it, and they would not dare ask. But they could always see the pain in her eyes when she saw a baby or heard about others having babies. This news could not be any better.

"Awww, congratulations, darling - how far along are you?" Asked Kika.

"Five weeks, apparently! It is still early days, but I just had to share it with my besties," she said, smiling.

Kika returned the smile, although she was a little concerned. She knew of many people who suffered miscarriages when they were under the 3-month mark. But then she shook her head - no way was that going to be Anita's story. She had been waiting for this moment for so long. God will not just take it away. She ignored her pessimistic thoughts and continued to celebrate with the other girls. Anita was finally going to be a mother, and that is all that mattered.

"We need to start planning your baby shower now! I'd do the honours," Mimi offered. Mimi was a well-known event planner. She planned Anita's wedding and had done many more elite events since then.

"Are you sure you're not too busy for my little baby shower, you know you're a 'big girl' in this Lagos. Are you sure you have time for me?" Anita jovially asked.

"Without #anatilove, I wouldn't be a 'big girl', so, anything for you gorgeous," Mimi said, tapping Anita on the nose with her index finger.

"Whatever you do, please do not forget that my wedding comes first," said Tara, folding her arms. This was typical of her to always make it about herself. Although she was happy that Anita was finally becoming a mother, she could not fathom why it had to be when she was getting married. After all, she had seven whole years for it to have happened. But she was used to Anita stealing her thunder.

Although Tara loved Anita and wanted the best for her, she knew she was jealous of her friend and resented her to an extent. Luckily, Anita truly valued her friendship with Tara, and although she did misbehave at times, Anita knew Tara had a good heart.

All the girls accepted Tara for who she was, but they were determined not to make this about her - so chose to ignore the comment.

"Girls, I've never felt so happy in my entire life, Nati's mother keeps calling me her daughter; I feel she is finally accepting me," Anita shrieked.

"Anita, why do you always need to seek approval from other people?" Kika asked, concerned. Anita was startled by Kika's comments, but she knew it was true. She usually had no problems with securing approval from others, and not being able to now was completely new to her. It made no sense why it had been so hard to similarly crack her husband's mother, whom she had known for over a decade.

"Kika, I don't seek approval, her liking me makes our family dynamics easier. You would understand when you become a wife," Although Anita agreed with Kika, she felt backed into a corner and therefore felt the need to attack Kika where she knew it would hurt - her single status.

"Okay, guys, that's enough," Mimi pleaded quickly to avoid escalation. Mimi was the designated peacemaker in the group and didn't want this incredible moment to be ruined for Anita. "In other news, I have a fashion show that I'd love to invite you guys to. I have VIP tickets, and the elites of the elites will be there. It's this Friday, would you guys like to come?"

The girls all looked at each other, "Yes!" They all screamed. This was one positive thing about having a friend in the event industry - freebies.

Mimi

"Where the hell have you been?" Rayo yelled, looking at Mimi disgustingly from head to toe.

"I just had brunch with the girls, you know every Sunday we have brunch," Mimi said, rolling her eyes at her husband.

"Do not roll your eyes at me, rude woman. You cannot be making impulsive plans, Mimi. You have a family!" Rayo snarled, "this is the last time I want to hear of such - do you hear me?"

Mimi nodded. What could she do? What Rayo says goes, and she just has to 'submit' like she always does. As Rayo left the living room in anger, Mimi dropped down onto the sofa, stretching her long legs out in front of her. She began to neatly braid her long natural hair into two French plaits, she soon started to wonder how she ended up in this position. She looked back on her life and thought about how she was raised in the perfect home. She had parents who loved each other deeply and who also loved her and her older brother, so chances of being in a loveless marriage was slim to none. She worked exceptionally hard in school, received good grades, and also had the best of friends. Love was not absent from Mimi's life. When it came to dating, she had many suitors who were brought up in the same social circle as herself, but Mimi was never attracted to them. She felt they had lived privileged lives, and some at the age of thirty still relied heavily on their parents' hand-outs for everything. Mimi had always been a hard worker - she was one of the top event planners in Lagos, Nigeria, and had been for many years. She desired a man with the same drive and ambition as her, someone who worked hard for his achievements and who was not overly comfortable living off of his parents.

This was why when she met Rayo two years ago, it was too good to be true. Mimi was the event planner for the annual NMA (Nollywood Movie Awards), and Rayo was one of the nominees for the Best Supporting Actor award. At the event, it happened that Rayo did not win, at which point he jumped up from his seat, made a scene, and left the auditorium. Mimi saw his reaction and was immediately consumed with concern for him, so much so, that she took the initiative to follow him outside. It was clear that Rayo was incredibly disappointed by his loss, and she hated to see him so crushed.

"Are you okay, sir?" She called out as she walked hastily towards him.

He tried his best to ignore her voice, but she caught up with him. Rayo tried not to look Mimi in the eye as he was tearing up; he had no idea who this woman was and did not want her to see his vulnerability.

"Sir, I am the event planner. You can trust me as I will never do anything to jeopardise this event." She was aware that Rayo probably might be thinking she was a reporter and so feel uncomfortable with her being around him.

"I'm fine," he said abruptly while wiping away his

tears. "I have worked so hard to try and make my life mean something, and I fail every single time."

"It's okay, I understand. Life can be tough," she said.

"This award was supposed to take me further in life. I need to put my siblings through school, I want to start my own company, but now I am back to square one. I am angry!" Rayo was surprised at how comfortable he felt expressing his inner feelings to Mimi. She made him comfortable - she seemed kind and understanding, and showed she was paying attention.

Mimi felt a similar connection, "I am so sorry to hear all of this. How about we can maybe grab a drink at the after-party?" She was not one to ask a man out, but there was something about Rayo, his struggles and vulnerability that made Mimi feel she needed to dig deeper.

"That sounds like a plan. I am Motunrayo Abraham - everyone calls me Rayo."

"I am Demilade Coker; everyone calls me Mimi," she laughed. Mimi found it interesting that they both had the coolest nicknames as first names. "Lovely to meet you."

At the after-party, Rayo and Mimi really hit it off, they spoke the whole night about everything - from how they grew up to where they wanted to be. Although their pasts were so different, their future seemed like it was heading in the same direction. This was everything Mimi had ever dreamt of in her future husband.

"Mimi, I have thoroughly enjoyed talking to you tonight," he said, smiling, "I know we just met, but I know that you are someone I would love to spend the rest of my life with."

Mimi was taken aback by how forward Rayo was, but she knew Rayo was stating the obvious. "I feel the same way, Rayo."

They exchanged numbers, and later that evening,

when they had gotten home, Rayo called her straight away to continue their conversation. Mimi discovered so much more about him. She found out he was twelve years older than her, that he grew up in a poor village and had to pay for himself to go to school, which is why he got into acting. He thought it would be an easy way to earn money on the side. She also found out that Rayo intended to start his own business, from which he could later take care of his family in the village. Mimi admired the fact that he took his life into his own hands and was making it happen. After a month of dating, Rayo asked Mimi to marry him at a candlelit dinner, precisely a month from the first day they met. Although Rayo did not have much money to start a family, he did what he could as he felt Mimi was worth it. After dessert, Rayo swiftly went on one knee and popped the question, and of course, Mimi said yes.

During that first month of them knowing each other, Mimi kept the relationship from her family as it was still early days. However, after she got engaged, she knew she could not leave them in the dark any longer, so declared the good news. To her surprise, they did not give her the reaction she was expecting. She was aware that they would probably all be in shock at the time frame, and she was ready for that, but instead, they started talking about Rayo's background and how it was so different from hers. But Mimi was a strong cookie and was not having any of that.

"Mimi, you have a successful business - do you feel marrying someone who has nothing, so quickly is the ideal scenario?" Says her overprotective brother.

"Mimi, has that boy even got a degree?" Says her egotistical father.

"Is he a man of God?" Says her spiritual mother.

"Mimi, he is using you for your money," says her very opinionated friend Kika.

"How old is he, my goodness?" Says all those around her.

Mimi was swift to put the naysayers in their place.

"I love him, and he loves me, and that is it!" She screamed back.

Six months later, Mimi had the wedding of her dreams, and although her family were against the marriage, they were supportive of her decision and contributed to the success of the wedding in every way they could.

After they got married, Mimi became pregnant with twin boys - Daniel and Desmond - very quickly, and her business continued to do very well. But soon after, Rayo began to show her an ugly side to him, which she wasn't aware he had. She soon discovered Rayo was disrespectful to those around him, including her. He tried his best to fit into Mimi's circle and lifestyle but always felt out of place. He ended his interest in acting and started an investment business, which he forcibly made Mimi put her savings into.

He would say, "we are married. It is not your money; it is our money."

Mimi was pregnant at this time and too tired to argue with him. She could see where he was coming from - he was her husband; it was not like he was running anywhere. After all, she did bring him into her world, and she needed to support him to ensure he did not feel inadequate. The only issue was that Rayo felt entitled to the proceeds of all Mimi's hard work, which really aggravated her.

So, what is Rayo's business?

Rayo is an addicted gambler, but will pose as running an investment company to get money off people. He would meet with the rich, some of whom happened to be Mimi's contacts, and tell them that he could turn their N100,000 into N500,000, for example; he delivered consistently and was seen as reliable by them. Soon, people began to trust him more and more with significant amounts. Mimi however, always felt that the business was too high risk, but was too petrified to tell anyone the truth. Rayo was dangerous, and she was scared that if she opened her mouth, he just might kill her.

Kika

Kika looked at her reflection in the mirror and ran her fingers through her long weave as she gazed at herself from head to toe. She was in high spirits as she waited for Femi, the guy she met at the restaurant, to pick her up from her apartment. They had been texting each other and talking on the phone non-stop since they met a week ago, and Kika was excited that he may be 'the one'.

She sat down once she got her outfit together and began to write in her journal.

'Dear God, I am about to go on a date tonight with Femi. Please can he be the one - I need this.'

Kika treated journaling as her way of speaking to God. She loved expressing herself through words. It gave her a chance to truly reveal everything in her mind, even if she was unsure of exactly how she was feeling. With the ups and downs in her relationships, she felt it was imperative to make God her best friend, and her journal was precisely the platform for doing that – communicating with her 'best friend'.

As she put her journal down on her side table, a message came through on her phone.

[Hi Kika, I am outside the building - should I come in?]

Kika rolled her eyes - was he serious? They just met, and he's already trying to pull some moves on her. "Strike one," she said to herself. She did not bother responding to the text; all she needed to know was that he was here. She grabbed her handbag and headed out of her building to the front gate.

"Hi, Femi!" Kika said, overly excited, hugging him.

"Hi Kika, I thought you would like me to come inside - I sent you a message. You look lovely, by the way?" He said, returning the hug.

"Oh, really? I only saw that you were outside and came out hurriedly. So sorry," Kika said, pretending she hadn't seen the full text message. She began to wonder why on earth she was apologising. "So, where are we off to?"

"Well, I was going to take you to this low-key spot in Victoria Island. They do seafood, which I know is your favourite. It is super romantic," Femi said.

Kika smiled. She loved the fact that Femi remembered how much she loved seafood. He put so much effort into the date, and Kika began to think that he must be the one.

As he drove them to the restaurant - Femi began to play some old school R&B jams - which was Kika's favourite too.

She laughed, "Wow, you have honestly been listening to everything I have said"

"Why wouldn't I?" He said, turning to the passenger-side to smile at her.

"Well, just so you know, this date is my treat," Kika said, remembering how he had paid for her and Daisy's meal.

Femi laughed, "You are not serious, how can I take you on a date and you pay for me? I want to treat you."

Kika knew that a lot of ladies would find this flattering. Anita and Tara most definitely love such chivalrous behaviour from the opposite sex; they even married such guys. But Kika just did not feel it was necessary; she found it fake. As soon as you marry a guy like this, you lose your individuality, and your identity becomes your husband's.

When they arrived at the restaurant, Femi did everything right. He opened all the doors for Kika and pulled out her chair as they were being seated.

"Femi, you are truly a gentleman," she said, smiling.

"Well, you are a lady, I need to treat you like one," he said.

Kika smiled. Maybe she needed to get these stereotypes out of her head and stop judging Femi. Maybe Femi was actually just a well-brought-up, nice guy.

"What will you be having?" Femi asked, kindly, as they looked at the menu, "I feel you would like the grilled shrimp."

Kika could not stop blushing, her mind began to travel. This had got to be what it felt like to be in love. She could not believe that she finally found 'The One' and boy, was he worth the wait.

Kika's phone began to ring. She looked at it and rolled her eyes when she saw who was calling.

"Is everything okay?" Femi asked, "Is it another guy?"

Kika looked at Femi, confused. "No," she chuckled. "Why would you think that - it's my boss. Sorry excuse me, I have to take this." She got up abruptly and headed to the front of the restaurant where it was a lot quieter, trying not to think about how weird it was for Femi to assume another guy was calling her.

"Kika, what took you so long to answer."

"Sorry, Ms Gozy; I am at dinner - is everything okay?" Kika asked.

"No, everything is not okay. I need you to come to the office now!" She yelled.

"...but Ms Gozy, it is Saturday, and I am at dinner with a friend."

"Kika! This is important - do you not value your position at 'Hello Lagos'?"

Kika put her hand on her forehead and let out a huge sigh, "I am on my way." She began to think to herself how Femi had planned such a beautiful date and how work had suddenly come to ruin it. "He's a gentleman; I'm sure he will understand." She said to herself.

As she headed back to her table, she saw Femi looking around the restaurant extremely uncomfortable.

'Don't worry, I haven't run away," she said, laughing.

Femi was relieved when he saw Kika heading back to their seat, "So what would you like to order" he said, trying to forget that Kika had just been on a long call.

"I have some bad news," Kika said, sitting down.

"What happened?" Femi asked.

"My boss just called me to tell me there is an emergency at work," Kika said apologetically.

"Oh no, what is the emergency?" Femi asked, concerned.

Kika looked confused; she realised she had not even asked Ms Gozy what the actual issue was.

"I am not too sure," Kika said, feeling stupid.

"Look, Kika, if you just aren't into this, please just say so," Femi said sternly.

"No, I am. But I just have to go. I am so sorry for ruining this beautiful planned night." She got up to hug Femi, and he gave her the cold shoulder. She had hoped Femi would offer to drop her at her office, but he seemed extremely irate that she was leaving. She did not dare ask.

"I am really sorry. I promise to make it up to you." She said, attempting to give him another hug.

Femi scowled and shrugged Kika off.

Kika was taken aback. She knew this was way out of line, but she did not feel it was enough for Femi to get so worked up. She was just as disappointed as he was.

She received a notification that her Uber was outside. She apologised one more time and made her way to the car. As she was driving out, she received a text from Femi.

Kika's heart sank as she read the words.

[I take my comment back about you being a lady. Enjoy your night with your 'boss']

Kika was confused. Was Femi implying that she was lying about going to meet her boss? She put her phone down with no intention of responding to the message.

"This guy needs to be a little bit more understanding," she said to herself. "Maybe I dodged a bullet."

She got out of the Uber and headed upstairs into Ms Gozy's office.

"What took you so long, Kika?" Ms Gozy said as Kika walked into the room

"Sorry Ms Gozy. I had to leave dinner and call a cab. I hope all is well?" Kika said, concerned.

"Well, there is an emergency - this article is going live tomorrow. I am torn about which image I should use with it," Ms Gozy walked towards Kika with the article and some images.

Was this a joke? Kika thought to herself. Was this the emergency she had to leave her date for?

She took the sheets of paper from Ms Gozy and began to read through the article. It was an article about the 'Up and Coming Musicians', and it was strangely similar to the one she had written - word for word.

"Oh, Ms Gozy, you decided to use my article," Kika

said sneering.

Ms Gozy laughed, "I would not say we used your article, dear. It definitely has my touch."

Kika looked through it and noticed the only change was that Ms Gozy had added an extra artist to the list. But everything else was word for word. Again, Ms Gozy belittles Kika as a writer, only to turn around and take all the glory for her work.

"So, what picture should I use?"

Kika could not believe this was why Ms Gozy brought her in. "Ms Gozy, was this the emergency?"

"Yes, Kika, why do you ask?" She said with a smirk.

"Ms Gozy, I was on a date, and you called me here for-"

"A date? Oh, I am so sorry that you think you are the only one who dates," she said sarcastically. "Kika, this is why when you tell me that you want to be promoted, I always look at you sideways. I am telling you we need to make some major decisions for an article, and you are telling me about your personal life? Please make it make sense."

Kika was aggravated, "- but Ms Gozy, could you not have emailed me the images?"

Ms Gozy rolled her eyes. "Next time, I will remember not to call you for important decisions - if that's what you want."

Kika kept quiet and shook her head. No, that was not what she wanted. But she also did not want Ms Gozy ruining her plans for stupid scenarios. She looked at the images that Ms Gozy showed. "I think you should go with this one on the right?".

Ms Gozy looked at the images - "hmm, I disagree, I am going with the other one."

Kika's blood began to boil. She gave Ms Gozy an

emotionless smile. What could she do? She most definitely could not call her out.

Kika got out of the shower and got her phone out to call Femi. She had hoped that Ms Gozy's antics would not have entirely ruined their potential.

"Hi, Femi, it's Kika."

"Can I help you?" Femi said rudely.

"Femi, I know you are angry, but please can I explain?"

"I don't want to hear it - whatever we were doing, it needs to stop. I don't date disrespectful women."

"- but, Femi!" Before Kika could finish, Femi had cut the call.

She looked out of her window and began to tear up. Was she ever going to be happy? Was her career ever going to take off?"

She brought out her journal and began to write.

Tara

"Hey babe, it's 11 pm, and you have been working on this all day. You need to take a break," Bode said, concerned while bringing Tara a glass of red wine into their home study.

"Thanks, dear, I am just finishing the hems on these samples. I have about six left to complete, and then I think I have a collection," Tara said excitedly. She was genuinely proud of the bold step she took in leaving her job at a law firm to focus on her fashion label, 'Tara Cole'.

Although it had not come easy, she was grateful for Bode. As a boyfriend turned fiancé, Tara felt Bode did a lot more than the average. He supported and encouraged her in her decision to leave her job and made her feel comfortable by providing her with the investment and useful contacts to get her started. He genuinely felt Tara was talented and hated seeing her work in law, which he knew she did not only dislike, but also prevented her from realising her full potential.

"These are coming together," he said, admiring the designs. "What is your plan once the hems are complete?" This was the real Bode Cole, the true entrepreneur, who always wanted to know one's next step.

"Well, maybe we should organise a photoshoot?" Tara wondered.

"Absolutely! I think marketing the brand and the collection is significant," he bent down to kiss Tara on the forehead, "I am so proud of you!"

Tara blushed and giggled.

"Since Dabira is coming in from the UK soon, we could potentially get her to model the clothing? She is built like a model," Bode said, believing he had come up with the smartest and most cost-effective plan.

"Erm no Bode, I would like top models in Nigeria, not ordinary people," Tara said, rolling her eyes.

"Well, she is pretty much your sister, and it will really cut down on costs," Bode said, thinking about the financials once again.

"Yes, well I didn't even think about that," Tara said laughing. "I love my cousin to bits and she is gorgeous. However, I want this to be done properly with top models. This is why we make such a great team, you will be lost without me."

Bode winked at her and left the room as Tara took a sip of her red wine. She was looking forward to finally making a name for herself.

"Tara Cole," she whispered to herself. She was excited

that the name was going to change her life. Becoming a wife - "Mrs Tara Cole" and a fashion brand "The Tara Cole" Her past of Tara Williams would soon be a distant memory.

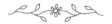

By the following morning, Tara had completed all the samples and was proud of every single piece. One of the items, in particular, was her favourite. It was maroon coloured, with puffy sleeves and lacing detail around the back. Tara was looking forward to the elite event that Mimi had invited her and the other girls to at their Sunday brunch. She thought maybe she could wear one of the gorgeous dresses she had designed and get general feedback from her friends about the collection.

"Bode, take a look at this," she said, walking into the study.

Bode looked at the dress and smiled. "It looks fantastic, babe, but why are you wearing it now?

"I am going to wear this to Mimi's event tonight. If I get positive feedback, I will tell people it is my collection, and there is more to come from it; if I get negative feedback, I will say I got it from abroad," Tara smiled, thinking she had it all figured out.

"No, Tara, you need to take a stand and be bold. You designed it, and you are proud of what you designed, right?" Bode said, starting to give her one of his routine motivational speeches.

"Yes I do love it, but -"

"No buts, Tara, you need to be confident in yourself. This is what people will read all over your face as you are wearing your outfit. So, rock it." Bode ended the conversation without giving Tara a chance to argue. "Look, we have couples counselling at church in an hour, are you ready?"

Tara sighed. She hated the couples counselling because this was where Pastor Jire and Pastor Lade Benson always, and were probably still going to give them both a stern talking to. Bode and Tara had not spoken about the issue of the wedding numbers and budgets since the incident a week ago, but Tara knew Bode would bring it up with the counsellors. He felt that there was no point going back and forth about it with Tara to avoid any arguments, but ironing it out with trained professionals and pastors was a healthy response.

Tara knew this approach was right, and because of this, their relationship went from strength to strength. She did, however, hate having to open up so much to these pastors about her life. She was afraid that one day they would discover something buried deep inside her that she would rather not have anyone know about - including Bode.

She put her kimono over her white vest top and jeans, looked over at Bode, and smiled.

"I'm ready babe, let's go."

Tara and Bode sat down in the counselling room with their hot drinks, waiting for Pastor Jire and Pastor Lade to come in for their session.

"If it isn't my favourite session of the week with my favourite couple," Pastor Jire said, coming into the room, so happy to see Tara and Bode.

"Oh, Pastor, I am sure you say that to everyone," Bode said, cracking up.

"Suck up," Tara said under her breath.

Tara kept a smile on her face, but behind her eyes, she was emotionless. Bode had grown up in this church, and they truly respected him as he had done so much for it. He had contributed to the construction of the church building; he had bought them offering baskets and had sponsored multiple events. Because of this, she felt no matter what issue they had; the pastors will always be inclined to take Bode's side and not hers.

"Okay, so how are you both doing?" Pastor Jire asked.

"Yes, we are doing great. A few ups and downs, but all in all, we are happy," Bode responded.

"What about you, Tara, you seem quite quiet, maybe a little sceptical?" Pastor Lade used her female instincts to assess the situation. She could see that Tara was on edge and not comfortable. She wanted to give Tara a chance to express how she feels.

"Yes, we are fine. No, I'm just looking forward to the session as well," Tara said, hoping Pastor Lade could not see through her lies.

"So, how is the wedding prep going?" Pastor Jire asked.

"Well, this is actually what we wanted to talk to you about, Pastor," Bode said.

"Oh, here we go," Tara said under her breath, hoping no one could hear her. Unfortunately, Pastor Lade did.

"I do not think Tara understands the importance of marriage. She is too focused on our wedding and outshining her friends. Pastors, we are way over our budget, she wants to invite almost a thousand people, and her funding solution is to make money off our friends by selling them overpriced Aso-Ebi. I mean, who does that?"

Both pastors looked over at Tara to see whether she had a response or whether she had a logical excuse.

"Yes, well, Bode is correct. I do not, however, see it as scamming my friends, though. I see it as a way to have the wedding of my dreams. I just thought it was a solution to the problem of 'we can't afford to feed all our guests'," Tara said, mimicking Bode.

The room went quiet, and although Tara was looking down at her shoes, she could feel all six eyes staring at her, piercing her soul. She looked up and caught Pastor Lade's gaze and how she smiled at her. This automatically calmed Tara down and made her feel a little bit more comfortable.

"Boys, can I please have a private conversation with Tara alone?" Pastor Lade asked.

Bode looked at the pastors and then at Tara, who had started staring at the floor again. He was apprehensive and taken aback as he thought the couple's counselling was speaking to the couple together and not individually. He, however, had no choice but to leave the counselling room and follow Pastor Jire out to his office.

"Tara, why do you want to have a wedding that you cannot afford?" Pastor Lade asked.

"First of all, Pastor, he can afford it. He is just being stingy. Plus, this is my dream. I have always wanted a luxury wedding where I am the star of the show, and people go out of their way just to be there."

"But Tara, you can have this without breaking the bank. You have to remember that once you both say 'I do', you and him will need to start to build a life together. If you spend it all on a wedding, what will you have left?" Pastor Lade tried to reason.

"I am not worried about that because Bode is incredibly wealthy, and I am about to start my fashion label, which will do exceptionally well too, so?" Tara said confidently.

"Tara, it is about saving for a rainy day - you never know what obstacles life will throw at you. Having a wedding for almost a thousand guests, many of whom you don't know, just so that you can be popular on the blogs is not wise at all. I am being honest. You and Bode's life together needs to be your priority."

Tara sighed, "I can see where you are coming from Pastor Lade, but if all my friends can throw lavish weddings and still be financially fine, why should I suffer and not throw mine?"

"Because Tara, you cannot afford it, and you don't even know if your friends could or could not afford it. Either way, no one should live beyond their means. They will regret it."

Tara could not understand why it always seemed like she was at the bottom rung of the ladder of life. Why was she never able to have the wedding or party of her dreams? Why couldn't she live her life to the max? Her peers have it so easy, and she has to suffer.

At this point, Pastor Lade could see in Tara's face that there was a lot more to this.

"Look, Tara, our time is up, but I am going to call you over the weekend, I feel we have a lot to talk about."

Tara quietly nodded while tears had started running down her face. Still keeping her head down, she got up and picked up her handbag with her back to Pastor Lade to avoid her seeing her tears. She quietly thanked her, and hurriedly left the room. As she was leaving, Bode and Pastor Jire were walking back in.

"Thank you so much for the session Pastor, see you next week," she said quickly. Before he could respond, Tara hurried to the car, hoping Bode could tell she was trying to leave as soon as possible - which he did.

"Is everything okay, babe?" he asked as soon as he got to the car to open it.

"Yes, everything is fine," she responded, getting into the passenger seat.

A journal to the reader

Dear Reader,

Ms Gozy knows that Kika will do just about anything to be associated with a brand like 'Hello Lagos'. She has mistreated her for years, and Kika still feels that this is where she needs to be in order to be successful.

Do you think God wants Kika to be here?

One could argue that maybe it is teaching her resilience. It is building her up. Well, this is true, perhaps it is. But Kika is not staying there because she feels God wants her to stay there. She is staying there because she has the fear that she would not be successful without being a part of this top company. She feels like she is set for life as long as she is a part of it. When in reality, she had been stagnant for years.

Do you ever plan your success without God's guidance? Do you ever feel you need to be friends with this person, hang out with this crowd, or go to this place to be happy or successful and get you to where you need to be?

Sometimes, God may have promised you something, but the avenue through which you get there may not be what you expect. Kika could easily have gone to a smaller Media House and grown from there, for example.

If you look at the life of Joseph (one of my favourite stories in the Bible - check it out in Genesis 37 - 45), he had a dream that all his brothers will bow down to him. The equivalent of us potentially having a dream to be rich and famous, for example.

Joseph was so excited about the dream that he went bragging about it to his brothers. He had no idea that he was going to be betrayed and left in a ditch, lied upon by Potiphar's wife, and end up in prison for all those years before he would get to the promise God made to him.

When I was in University studying Architectural Design & Technology, I was so desperate to be a residential Interior

Designer. In fact, my dissertation was about home interior design. I was so sure that this was what God wanted me to do that I even ended up starting a blog about it. Once I graduated, I went to Florence, Italy, to do a Masters' in Interior design and had planned my portfolio as perfectly as I could to ensure I got a job as soon as I got back to London. That was my plan.

I finished my Masters' at the end of May but had already started applying for jobs from the end of March. I kid you not; I applied to over 300 residential interior design companies. Some companies even asked me how I found them; that is how deep my research went. I received only one interview, and I did not get the job.

I was so distraught because I felt I had planned my life perfectly. I knew God wanted me to be an interior designer, so why wasn't I getting a job role in it? It made no sense.

This takes me to Jeremiah 29:11 "For I know the plans I have for you," declares the LORD, "plans to prosper you and not to harm you, plans to give you hope and a future".

God promised me that I would be an interior designer, not necessarily a residential one, as I thought. What next? I applied for one commercial role after I had been unsuccessful at the other 300 residential ones, and guess what, I got an internship straight away, which led to my very first interior design job role. Now, five years later, I am loving commercial design, and I no longer see myself in the residential sector.

Actually, I had a taster, and I hated it, but that's a story for another day.

The point I am trying to make is sometimes we feel like we all have it figured out. We have a plan, and we believe we know where we are going and how to get there. The truth is we have no idea.

If God really wants you to be in an uncomfortable situation for growth, you would know he wants you to be there because you will have peace about it.

Journal Task 2: Take a moment to think about where you are at this moment, and where you would like to be. Write down the steps you feel you need to take to achieve them. Think about emotional steps as well as the physical steps you need to take. Now leave them in God's hands by praying this prayer.

'Dear Lord, these are my desires, and these are the avenues I believe I should take to achieve them. Please let it be known if they are not part of your will, and allow my heart to be open to your ideas. Amen.'

Tip: If you are uncomfortable in a situation in your life, make sure you confirm your motives as to why you are staying. If you are in a relationship you feel isn't right, are you scared of being alone? Are you worried that you may never find someone?

Lots of Love X

Simi Alexis Romeo

CHAPTER THREE

Mimi

"Hey, I am going to drop the boys off with my mother, and then I am off to the fashion event," Mimi said nervously to Rayo in their living room. He was reading a newspaper, smoking cannabis, while simultaneously drinking a glass of whisky. This is something Rayo did every night without fail.

"When were you planning on telling me that you were going out tonight?" Rayo asked without even looking up from his paper.

"Rayo, I told you last month I was going to this event," Mimi pleaded. "Can't you remember?"

"How much will you be making from it?" Rayo asked while taking a sip from his drink. He was always keen to know precisely how much Mimi was making from every event she had. He knew that whatever she made was his, and if she lied about it, he would hurt her. She was fully aware of this, so she always remained open and honest.

"N4.5 million," She said, looking down at her feet.

"Woah!" Rayo looked up from his paper. "That is a lot of money, man," he began to laugh uncontrollably, "I have plans for it!"

"What sort of plans?" She said impulsively, immediately regretting it.

"Ahn Ahn, you are so greedy, is it your business?" He continued to laugh.

The way Rayo spoke baffled Mimi. Yes, it was her business which she had before he was even in the picture. And if he wanted to take the money she made, it was her business how he intended to spend it. Rayo would either gamble with the money he takes from her or will use it to replace clients' money that he would lose.

"Anyway, you'd better get going before we lose all our fees," he laughed as he took another sip from his glass.

Mimi scowled, left the house and made her way to the event. The change in Rayo from a loving suitor and groom to this monster who controls, abuses, and frightens her, is one of the most incomprehensible things Mimi had ever experienced in her life. If only she had listened to her family members and spent more time getting to know Rayo. She would have taken his flaws a lot more seriously.

She thought back to when they had met at the NMA's and how Rayo reacted when he did not win the award.

"He's always been like this," she mumbled to herself. Mimi shook her head and tried to gear herself up to be in a good mood as she was going to see her best friends Tara, Anita, and Kika. She did not want them to suspect a thing.

"Well done, team, the space looks phenomenal. Remember your cues that we discussed during the rehearsal, now go forth and be great," Mimi was always great at giving the best pep talks to her team before an event. She believed it encouraged them. The fashion show event was all set up, and the music started to take over the entire room.

"Mimi!" Kika screamed from behind her.

Mimi turned around, trying to locate the sound that was about to make her go deaf. "Wow, Kika, I am impressed. The first one to arrive." She leant forward to give her a big hug and a kiss on either cheek. "You look great!"

"Well, what can I say? I have come to support my bestie and have to dress the part," she said, twirling and laughing.

Mimi laughed; she loved being around Kika. Kika had this jovial spirit that could light up anyone's day. She was very quick to support her friends. Out of the whole friendship group, Kika was the only one yet to be married or close to marriage, and she knew it affected her. Kika hated going to events on her own. If only she knew what it was like to be in a marriage but actually be alone all the time, like her situation.

"So, how is work?" Asked Mimi.

"It's great!" Kika said, trying to mask her real emotions.

Mimi was aware that Kika was struggling at work but also knew that she pretty much worshipped this job and accepted all sorts of mistreatment from her boss. Mimi felt it was clear that Kika did not value herself.

"Look, I know you love your job very much, but you are so talented, Kika. I feel you can do so much more. You write in your journal every night and have this passion for women being secure in themselves. Why don't you do something with that?" Mimi said.

Kika smiled. She knew Mimi was right.

"That is definitely something I need in my life," Mimi continued looking towards the ground.

"Why, what is going on?" Kika could tell that Mimi was not happy, especially within her marriage. You could see it written all over her face every time the conversation turned to Rayo. However, because Mimi fought against everyone's objections to walk down the aisle with Rayo, she was too proud to now admit that she was not happy. "Is Rayo coming tonight?" She went on to ask.

"No, he had a work thing. Let me show you to your seat before the other ladies show up," she said, changing the subject.

At that moment, Tara walked in, and Mimi could not be happier to see her.

"Wow, Tara! You look amazing!" Kika said, "what are you wearing?"

"Hey, girls!" She hugged Mimi and Kika intensely, "none other than *moi* - The Tara Cole Collection."

Mimi and Kika both looked at Tara in awe. They brought out their phones and started recording her to put on their social media story.

Kika started, "Hey, everyone, can you just look at my gorgeous friend, Tara soon-to-be Cole wearing her own design."

Mimi quickly continued, "When can we get our hands on one of these amazing dresses, Ms Tara Williams-Cole?"

"It is coming soon - so stay tuned," she said, laughing.

As soon as the girls put their phones away, Tara suggested they should walk the red carpet. "I think it will be nice to have professional pictures taken," she said.

"I think we should wait for Anita to come, it will be quite unfair to take pictures without her," Kika defended.

"Well, that is what you get when you come late," Tara responded.

"She is pregnant, plus you only just walked in your-self," exclaimed Kika.

"Okay, the two of you, please stop it," Mimi said sternly. She could see where this was going, Tara was always quick to pick up on Anita's faults, and Kika was always ready to defend her. There was no point - at the end of the day, they were all friends and had been for many years.

"Hi girls, sorry I'm late," Anita screamed. She walked in wearing this gorgeous white maxi dress.

Mimi and Kika rushed to her side, while Tara slowly made her way with a plastered grin.

"Anita, you are glowing - wow pregnancy looks good on you," said Kika stroking the curls in her hair.

"I wish I looked this good when I was pregnant," Mimi continued.

"Such suck-ups," Tara whispered under her breath. She could see Anita was glowing, but she could not stand how the attention suddenly shifted from her self-made outfit to Anita's glowing skin - which in reality had not changed much as far as she was concerned, from even before she was pregnant.

"Right girls, let's walk the red carpet and then take our seats quickly - the show is about to start," Mimi said.

The girls walked the red carpet, posing, answering questions, and making jokes with the interviewers. They were naturals - this was one of the reasons Mimi loved having them all there. Once they had finished, they made their way to their front row seats to watch the show.

As the models walked down the runway, the ladies clapped and showed tremendous support. They were inspired by the designs that had come out. This was espe-cially true for Tara as an aspiring fashion designer.

"Mimi, this time next year, you will have my collection on this runway," Tara said.

Mimi laughed, "of course, why not?"

Anita smiled and turned to Mimi, who was sitting right beside her. But her smile abruptly switched to a concerned look. With all the stage lighting at the event, Anita was able to see marks under Mimi's makeup, which she had obviously tried to cover up. Mimi noticed Anita looking at her and quickly turned the other way.

"What is that, Mimi?" Anita whispered sternly.

"Anita, concentrate on the show, everything is fine."

"Mimi, no amount of foundation can cover up that scar I see under your eyes." She paused. "Did he do this to you?"

"Who is he?" Mimi pretended not to know who Anita was referring to.

"Rayo!"

"He is my husband who loves me dearly, he will never do such a thing - please let's get back to the show," Mimi snapped.

Anita did not want to, but she had to let it go - it was neither the time nor the place, but she will surely be looking to get to the bottom of this at a more appropriate time.

Tara

Tara got home at around 2 am after the fashion show. She tried not to wake Bode up as she knew he was getting up very early the next day to pick her cousin, Dabira, up from the airport. Although the night went very well, and people loved her outfit, she did end up feeling less than her peers once again.

Anita walked in late with her pregnancy glow and ended up stealing the show. Tara loved Anita, but she was fed up with Anita stealing her shine. She was fed up with things not going the way she wanted them to go. Why couldn't she just walk in a room and command attention as Anita did? She always felt she had to work ten times harder to prove herself. She was sure that Anita could come into an event wearing jeans and a plain white t-shirt while she could come in wearing a designer gown, and all eyes will still be on Anita.

She carefully took off her dress and hung it up for dry cleaning. Afterwards, she went into her ensuite bathroom to have a shower and get ready for bed. While brushing her teeth, Tara felt a deep sadness in her heart. She tried to replay her day to pinpoint what exactly was depressing her.

She thought about how that morning, she was so happy that her sample collection had been completed, and how much of a great achievement that was. Tara then remembered the counselling session with Bode and the Pastors and how emotional she felt. She still did not understand why that conversation would bring her down. Lastly, she remembered dressing up to go to the event. She felt happy and excited, leaving the house wearing her 'Tara Cole' outfit, such that Bode did not want to let her out of his sight. Once she got to the event, her friends were excited to see her, and they would not stop going on about how beautiful she looked and how gorgeous the dress was. She even remembered the shock on Kika and Mimi's face when she told them she had designed and made it herself. However, as soon as Anita walked in, everything changed. All they could talk about was how Anita was 'glowing' and how 'pregnancy looked good on her'. And although she knew it did, she could not understand why everyone was so quick to forget about her.

Tara spat out the last bit of toothpaste, rinsed her brush and mouth, and then stared at herself in the mirror.

"What is wrong with me?" She asked herself. She put on her pyjamas, went to lie in bed, and slept off.

As Tara woke up the following morning at about 6 am, she noticed Bode putting on his shoes in readiness to go and pick up Dabira from the airport.

"Morning, my love," she said to Bode yawning.

"Hey sweetheart," he leant over to give her a morning kiss and immediately screwed up his face in mock disgust as he smelt her morning breath. "Eww," he said, sticking out his tongue.

"Sorry, I did not beg you to kiss me this morning," she responded, laughing.

"How was last night?" Bode said to her whilst wiping his mouth with his fist.

Tara sighed, "Well, it went well, I guess."

"Just well? Did your friends like your dress?" Bode asked, concerned.

"Yes, they did. They loved it!"

"So what is this problem, you don't seem yourself?" Bode said, staring into Tara's eyes.

Tara felt she could never really express her love-hate relationship with Anita. She did not want to be a jealous friend, because deep down, in all honesty, she wanted the best for her friend. When Anita was unable to have children, Tara actively prayed that she would. When Anita got married, Tara was the most helpful and kindest bridesmaid, as she waited on Anita, hand, and foot. It was just a feeling that Anita always had everything handed to her so easily, and no matter how hard Tara worked, she always lost the 'competition' that she had created in her head.

"I just felt there was not as much attention on my outfit. People were more concerned about other things."

Bode looked shocked, "What other things?"

"Well, Anita and her glowing skin," she said while looking down at the floor in shame.

Although it had never been discussed, Bode could always see how Tara's friendship with Anita seemed strange and how at times, Anita's achievements will bring Tara down.

"Look, babe, you are such a diamond to me, and everyone around you. Plus, Anita really loves you, and I am sure if you speak to her about how you are feeling, she would understand."

Tara looked at Bode with confusion. She did not see why Anita needed to know about the jealousy that she felt for her. It was not necessarily Anita's problem - she was just significantly blessed, and that was not her fault. In reality, would Anita want to have a friend that was jealous of her? She would probably withdraw from her, and Tara really valued their friendship.

"I love you, babe, one last kiss before you leave," she said, giggling, trying to kiss him.

He tried to escape but conveniently lost the battle and kissed her before he left for the airport.

Later that morning, Tara showered and got ready for the day. She was cooking breakfast when her phone began to ring from an unknown number.

"Hello?" Tara said suspiciously.

"Good morning Tara, this is Pastor Lade."

Tara rolled her eyes - this lady did not waste any time contacting her.

"Good morning, Pastor Lade. How are you?"

"I am well, thank you, Tara - I think we should talk

about yesterday and how you were feeling." Pastor Lade sounded uncomfortable.

"Well, to my surprise, I am feeling a lot better," Tara said, pushing to get Pastor Lade off the phone.

"That is great to hear. Now, you are going into a season of marriage, and marriage is tough. You want to ensure as much as possible that you are ready so you avoid mishaps in your marriage.

"Yes, absolutely!" She said sarcastically.

"Tara, everyone has struggles they go through. I always say it's either you are coming out of a struggle, currently in a struggle, or about to go into a struggle - we all face it."

"Yes, Pastor Lade, I agree," she said, looking at her watch.

"In fact, in John 16:33, Jesus said that in the world, you will have trials and tribulations, but guess what? He said to be of good cheer, that he has overcome the world."

"Oh, wow, yes." Tara felt bad and was hoping Pastor Lade would not sense her sarcasm, but she honestly did not want to talk about any of this.

"So Tara, what will you say are some of the trials that you have experienced?"

She rolled her eyes, "erm, I am not sure." Tara thought about the question, she thought about how her mother abandoned her and how she was shuffled from home to home. She thought about her desire to be celebrated and her struggle with always losing battles. But no way was she going to bring up any of these with Pastor Lade. Even Bode did not know the extent of these pains she struggles with daily.

"Hello, Tara, are you there?"

"Yes, Pastor Lade, I am. I am so sorry I need to go, Bode went to pick my cousin up from the airport, and they have just come through the gate. We can continue this chat at our session next week."

"Oh okay, can we at least pray - "

At that moment, Tara ended the call. She felt bad, as she never wanted to be in a position where she would disrespect an elder in the church, but Tara did not know Pastor Lade and talking to her about what she was going through was something she was not ready for.

She hurried outside to meet Dabira and Bode.

"Dabira, Dabira!" Tara screamed as she rushed to her cousin to give her a big hug.

Dabira reciprocated the excitement and ran towards Tara. "I have missed you, sis. Mum misses you so much, too."

Tara began to cry. "I have missed both of you very much, too."

Bode was so happy to see Tara in great spirits. He knew how much she and Dabira loved each other, and he loved seeing her so happy, especially because she was a bit down earlier.

"Right girls, let's go inside, the sun is too hot," Bode said, carrying Dabira's luggage into the house.

They laughed and followed Bode inside.

"I have made you your favourite - some good old yam, eggs and corned beef," Tara said excitedly.

Dabira laughed, "Oh sis, you know me too well, that sounds perfect."

A journal to the reader

Dear Reader,

If anyone had a friend like Tara, they should seriously be concerned and wary. A friend like her, who is jealous of you, can be terrifying to have. In this day and age, society will tell you to cut such 'friends' off, especially as they cannot be thought to have your best interest at heart.

To an extent, I agree. However, is it that black and white? Is there a grey area?

When you get to know the struggles Tara is facing - the battle of abandonment by her own mother or the fact she always feels oppressed by others - you can see that her behaviour stems from something very deep.

I think it is important to understand that hurt people, hurt people. Tara is hurt, and her closest friends can see that she isn't all bad. She does have a good heart, but her flaws can be hurtful.

Imagine if her friends chose to cut her off, she would end up dealing with even more abandonment issues, reinforcing the cycle of despair.

Yes, you can argue that the Bible says 'cut off the branches that bear no fruit'. Well, actually, it says 'He cuts off every branch in me that bears no fruit...' John 15: 2.

In other words, it is not your decision, God puts people in your life for a reason and a season and HE will pull them away from you naturally if He feels those relationships bear no fruit.

You have to bear in mind that nobody is perfect, not even you. If God has put people in your life, it is for a reason. You have to remember that God plans everything about you in your life. Every single detail.

I am not condoning being in a physical or emotionally abusive relationship. If someone is hurting you in that way, I'd say run. There is no reason God wants you to be in that sort of envi-

61

ronment. Remember Jeremiah 29:11- "...plans to prosper you and not to harm you, plans to give you hope and a future."

I was a massive advocate for cutting people off. I used to say stuff like 'They don't deserve me', 'I don't see the value of them in my life', 'They are not good friends to me so why should I keep them around'. God made me realise that that is incredibly selfish. What if they deserve me, what if they see the value in me, what if I am a good friend to them, and they should keep me in their life.

God may want to use me for something they are dealing with in their lives. If I was more focused on God than my own feelings, I'd probably see the bigger picture. This is why it is always important to ask God for guidance in these situations. If you decide to cut off something prematurely without his guidance, there is a high chance you would regret it.

Another thing to consider is whether you are the 'Tara' in your friendship group. You mean well, but you cannot control the jealousy that creeps up when others are progressing in life. Sometimes you could be like Tara, and have experienced something within your childhood that causes you to react in a negative way. It is not your fault and does not make you a bad person. However, do not victimise yourself. Acknowledge your hurt and pain and where it stems from. It could be a feeling of rejection, abandonment or a negative experience. Once you acknowledge the pain, pray against comparison and try to be thankful of where God has placed you at this time. I am sure you can find so many things to be grateful for.

Journal Task 3: Write down a list of people in your life that you may see or speak to regularly. Write down how you could be a blessing to them and what you could offer them. We are taking the spotlight off of ourselves and focusing on others.

Tip: Are there people in your life you have cut off prematurely? You may still not have peace about it. Time may have passed, and it is awkward. Pray for them like you were praying for yourself. For example. "Lord give them success, keep them happy, make them joyful" God will begin to soften your heart towards them.

Lots of Love X

Simi Alexis Romeo

CHAPTER FOUR

Mimi

"Hello my baby, how are you today?" Mimi said, lifting Desmond out of his crib. Daniel was still fast asleep, which was a relief for Mimi. It was Sunday afternoon, which meant her nannies had their day off. The twins had both been fast asleep, and Mimi had been dreading them waking up at the same time, as she knew they would both wake up hungry, and it would be hard to focus on them individually.

Mimi felt like a single mother, raising her twins. Rayo was never available to help out in the home, and he was always out, smoking, drinking, and most likely hanging out with other women. Mimi turned a blind eye to it all and did her best to focus on her work and her children.

As Desmond was comfortably feeding, she heard her phone ringing through her AirPods. She rolled her eyes at the interruption as this was the time of the day she usually took out to relax and bond with her babies. Mimi carefully took her hands out from under the feeding blanket to reach for her phone and see who was calling - it was Anita. She was hesitant to answer the phone because she knew what Anita was calling about - her bruised eye. She had done her best to cover the mark as much as possible, and she felt she did an excellent job. In fact, Rayo would not have let her leave the house if the bruises were visible. Trust Anita and her nurturing ways to always look beneath the layers. Mimi was also hesitant because Rayo was upstairs, and if he heard her discussing the bruise, she might get another bruise.

She sent Anita's call to voicemail and proceeded to send her a text message.

[Hey girl, I am feeding the boys at the moment - can I call you back? Mimi]

A few moments later, Anita responded.

[Sure, hun! I was calling to tell you that I am round the corner from your house. I would love to pop by to see you and the boys. It will give me great baby practice. (Wink Emoji)]

Mimi thought about it. In a few minutes, she knew she would need help with the boys, especially when Daniel woke up. "I'll just avoid any conversation regarding Rayo," she thought to herself. Mimi responded to Anita, [Sure hun. X]

"Hey dear," Rayo said, walking into the living room. It seemed like he was leaving the house to go, God knows where, but Mimi most definitely was not going to ask him. "How are you?" he said whilst hugging Mimi and then kissing Desmond on his forehead. This was about the sweetest Rayo had been to Mimi in a while. Mimi was happy because it seemed like he was in a good mood, and it was probably the perfect time to let him know Anita was coming to visit.

"So, Anita is coming round. She wanted to see the boys. I told you she is pregnant now?"

"Wow, seriously?" He said, surprised, "I am happy for her and Nati. They deserve it."

"Yes, they do. Where are you going?" She questioned apprehensively.

"I am going to meet up with Nati and Bode and a few of the other boys for a drink," he said, putting on his blazer.

Mimi suddenly began to twist her afro, something she does when she feels uncomfortable. She was worried Rayo was going to exploit them for money.

She sighed.

If anything happened, she would bail him out as usual - she was sure of that.

"Okay, well, have fun and don't do anything that I wouldn't," she said nervously.

After Rayo left, it was not long before Anita walked in.

"Hey, girl!" Mimi shrieked with excitement as Anita hugged her.

"Aww, look at the handsome fellas. So cute!" She said, admiring Desmond, who was peacefully laying on Mimi's chest and Daniel, who was still in the crib.

"Mimi, we missed you at brunch today," Anita said concerned.

"Yes, well, I had so much to do," she lied. Rayo had forbidden her from going to the weekly brunches, and she was not going to let the girls know that.

"Has Rayo gone to meet with Nati?" Anita asked.

"Yes, he said he is meeting up with them for a drink," Mimi explained.

"A drink? More like the biggest business deal in life. Apparently, Rayo has this billion Naira idea that is going to make the whole of Fawun Investments super-rich. Any clue on what this is?" Anita questioned.

"Oh, really?" she laughed nervously.

Anita looked at Mimi, and she could see there was something she was not telling her. She quickly sent a text message to Nati without Mimi's knowledge.

[Do not take the deal. With Mimi now and something is off]

Anita never really trusted Rayo, and it was quite clear that there was some sort of abuse happening in the Abraham's household.

"How is your eye?" Anita asked.

"I can see," Mimi responded sarcastically.

"Mimi, I know he is hurting you - what is going on? I am your friend; you should tell me!"

"Shh!" Mimi whispered in fear. She knew her husband was crazy, and she has no idea how far the craziness could take him. For all she knew, he could have had their whole house bugged and wired. Especially because he was so calm with Anita coming to visit.

"I am fine, Anita! Leave it!" She whispered.

The tension was broken when Daniel at that moment woke up from sleep and started crying. Mimi carefully passed Desmond over to Anita, so she was free to start feeding Daniel.

"Let's talk about how you are about to be a new mum!" Mimi said positively changing the subject.

"Oh absolutely," Anita played along. However, she was still seriously concerned.

Later that evening, Mimi was putting the boys to bed when she heard a loud thud that came from downstairs.

She rushed to the upstairs foyer and peeped through the ironmongery fence, to see Rayo coming into the house drunk. He had that glazed look in his eyes, and she knew what that look meant. She locked the boys in their nursery. She knew Rayo would never hurt them, but she would not put anything past him when he was drunk.

"MIMI!!!" She heard him scream. She ran to her bedroom to wear layers of clothing - if he was going to touch her, she needed to ensure she did everything to soften the blows at least, as much as possible.

"Mimi!" He screamed again. She took a deep breath and slowly came out of the room and made her way downstairs.

"Hey, hunny, are you okay?" She said, trying to keep her voice as calm as possible whilst keeping her distance from him.

"What the hell did you say to Anita?" He screamed at her.

She was confused. She was so sure she was careful not to say anything she felt could backfire. Rayo began to walk towards her. She was so petrified that she began to stutter, "what do you mean? - I said nothing."

"DO NOT LIE TO ME!" He yelled, throwing a slap across her face that made her fall to the ground.

"I ***SLAP*** WAS ***KICK*** ABOUT ***SLAP*** TO ***SLAP*** MAKE ***KICK*** SERIOUS ***PUNCH*** MONEY ***SLAP*** TODAY ***PUNCH*** AND YOU RUINED IT!" Rayo yelled, worn out.

"Please stop! Please, Rayo," Mimi cried.

He sat on the floor next to where Mimi laid shaking uncontrollably.

"I am going to ask you one more time, what did you say to Anita because Nati was all for the deal and all of a sudden, he wasn't."

At this point, Mimi realised that Anita must have observed her awkwardness about the deal and probably let Nati know immediately. However, she had no idea how she was going to escape from this. She honestly did not tell Anita anything, but she knew if she told Rayo that, he would not believe her.

She gulped, "Rayo, please hear me out. Anita asked me about the deal, and I told her I knew nothing about it, because Rayo, you do not tell me anything. Nati and Anita tell each other everything. The fact I did not know may have made Anita nervous about it." Mimi let out a quiet sigh, and Rayo looked at the ceiling, thinking about her explanation.

"Hmm, I guess that makes some sort of sense," Rayo said.

She was quite impressed by how quickly she came up with that explanation, but desperate times do call for desperate measures.

"Maybe I should start to tell you things," he said, laughing. "Go and clean yourself up, and let's go to bed."

Mimi quickly got off the floor and ran to the bathroom. She began to slowly clean her wounds, trying to avoid the sting. "Oh, God, why am I going through what I am going through?" She whispered. "What did I do to deserve this?" She wept uncontrollably.

She was at breaking point. Rayo constantly disrespected her, physically and mentally abused her, and stole from her. She was becoming depressed, and she could see her entire life collapsing around her.

"I am trapped," she whispered to herself. "I cannot just leave; he would kill me, my family, and hurt our boys as he has threatened in the past." Mimi was scared. She was brought up to be a strong, independent woman, but Rayo did not let her be. She was made to feel she was dependant on a man, when in reality, she provided all the money. "God, I know we don't speak that much, but I ask you, please get me out of this situation. Please protect my children. Help me!"

Once she finished cleaning herself up, she put on a fresh set of pyjamas and made her way to the bedroom.

"I need to nurse the boys, so I will be in the nursery," she said to Rayo. She was lying. "She knew she did not want to be anywhere near him.

"Well, I wanted to have some 'couple' time, but fine, go and feed the rascals," he said, turning his back to her and laying on his right side, to instantly fall asleep.

Mimi thought to herself that this man was mad and delusional. "You literally just beat me black and blue, and suddenly you want to have some 'couple time' " she said under her breath.

Mimi left their bedroom and made her way to the boy's nursery. She let herself back into the room and locked the door securely. While laying on the sofa, she found it hard to sleep. She needed a way out, but she did not know how.

Anita

It was 2 a.m. when Anita snapped awake to hear whispers coming from the ensuite bathroom.

At first, she thought she was possibly hearing things and was still deep in sleep. However, the voice became a lot more prominent and was slightly chilling. She rubbed her growing belly and reached out to the right side of the bed to alert her husband about the strange thing happening in their bathroom. But Anita was taken aback to find he wasn't there.

She slowly lifted herself to a sitting position, quite baffled as to where he could be. She then carefully raised the duvet to get herself out of bed and slowly approached the bathroom, noticing that the door had been left slightly ajar. She peeked through the gap and saw Nati pacing up and down the bathroom on the phone, looking stressed.

Anita was confused as it was unlike Nati to be awake in the middle of the night, let alone to take phone calls - he loved his sleep.

"Look, I can't speak right now... Because I am with my wife and it's two in the morning, I will call you tomorrow," Nati said assertively.

Anita could not hear who was on the other end of the call, but she could hear a mumble in a high-pitched tone - who on earth could he be talking to?

"I'm so sorry, we will sort it out tomorrow," Nati dismissed the caller.

Anita was sure something untoward was going on. Could Nati seriously be speaking to a woman at this time of the night? During their entire relationship, Nati had never given Anita a single reason not to trust him. It would not make sense for this to be changing when they were finally becoming parents.

"Okay, okay, bye." Nati dropped the phone and sat on the edge of the bathtub. He let out a huge sigh and dropped his face in the palms of his hands, and waited for a moment. Anita was genuinely concerned as to what could be stressing her husband out. He never really expressed when he was stressed out or anxious about anything. He always felt it was essential to lead the household the best way he knew how - by never being seen to be vulnerable.

She saw Nati stand up abruptly and take large strides towards the bathroom door. It took Anita a moment to realise she was about to be caught spying, and she quickly turned around to make a hurried leap back into bed, carefully holding her belly. The bathroom door swung open just as Anita had finished tucking herself into bed. She knew it was not the right time to question Nati about the phone call, and she did not want him to know she had been eavesdropping.

Nati did not suspect a thing as he was still bewildered from the phone call. He did not even hear Anita trying to catch her breath from moving so quickly. All he knew was how his heart would not stop beating louder and faster. When he got to his side of the bed, he meticulously lifted the duvet and gently slid into bed, trying not to wake his newly pregnant wife. He rested on his back, looked up at the ceiling, and began to bite his lips.

"Nati, you've really messed up big time," he thought to himself. The tension in the bedroom was so strong that Anita felt she needed to be there for her husband, no matter what. She faced him and rested her hand on his prickly chest. She wanted him to know she was there for him no matter what the issue was. Nati grasped her hand and turned to look over at her, and then they locked eyes".

"I'm sorry, baby, did I wake you," he whispered.

"It's fine, love," she stroked his face with her fingers, "Is everything okay?" She asked concerned, trying not to let loose on the fact she had heard him on the bizarre phone call.

"Yes, everything is fine, hun," he dismissed, "let's get some sleep; it's extremely late." He kissed Anita on the forehead, turned over, and went to sleep. But it was not that easy for Anita to let it go. She anxiously closed her eyes to try to sleep, but the mysterious phone call, unfortunately, continued to play in her mind, over and over again.

It was morning, and Anita was still focused on the events of last night. She did not know how to bring it up with Nati. He hated it when she pried for information or refused to believe him when he tells her that everything is fine. He felt Anita should not get into 'men's issues', and she should just take care of herself and be the lady of leisure she was, rather than worry about the things that were of no concern to her.

She felt she desperately needed some counsel, and out of her friendship group, Kika was the only one whom she felt she could trust regarding such deep issues. They had known each other the longest, and their mothers had grown up together. Both mums went to the same school, got married, and had Kika and Anita around the same time, and they were not only best friends but were also like sisters.

Although Kika was not in a relationship and had never been married, Anita always felt Kika was significantly blessed at giving really good advice about relationships. She knew when Kika becomes a wife, she would probably have the best marriage.

Anita picked up her phone to call Kika.

"Hey Anita, I'm in a meeting, can I call you back?"

Anita rolled her eyes and sighed, "sure."

"Are you okay?" Kika asked, concerned after hearing the emotion in Anita's voice.

Anita was used to the fact that her friends appeared to be too busy to talk on the phone during the week. She understood the reasons behind it, they had up and coming businesses, demanding jobs, or families to raise. They did not have time to sit and talk for hours like they did when they were in university. This was why Anita was adamant they all make time to meet for their weekly Sunday brunches. She did not want to lose any of her friends.

In the time Anita had been unable to have children, being a housewife had become dull and lonely. She had desired to start multiple businesses, but Nati would always be against it. He would tell her to "go and get pampered at the spa" or "go to a yoga class". He was adamant that he did not want his wife to work. He wanted her to always be available to him, which was never an issue for Anita initially, but had slowly become a problem over the years.

"Yes I'm fine Kika, I just need to talk to you about something very important," Anita sounded very stressed like she was on the verge of tears.

"Oh," Kika said with concern. "Well, in that case, why don't we meet up at your favourite restaurant tonight, have a few drinks - well maybe some tea for you." Kika chuckled, attempting to cheer Anita up.

Anita let out a soft giggle. "Yes, that would be great. I will meet you at half seven."

"Hi, reservation under Mrs Anita Fawun Edoh, please, table for two," Anita said very proudly.

She loved saying her full name and showing the world she was married to the incredible Mr Nati Edoh. She was dressed to seriously impress. Anita rarely went out at night; therefore, her casually meeting a friend for drinks was not to be taken lightly.

She followed the hostess to their reserved table right near the window, just as she liked it. She ordered a virgin mojito for herself and a long island iced tea for Kika - it was her favourite. Anita sat on her phone, scrolling through social media. Kika was running late, but it was something Anita was used to.

Fifteen minutes later, Kika came barging into the

restaurant, flustered. "So sorry I'm late, after our call, my boss pulled me in for a chat. She said that I'm losing my mojo." Kika hissed, "why wouldn't I lose my mojo, she gives me no freedom to be creative and treats me like her assistant." Kika saw the long island iced tea on the table and smiled, "you see this is why I need people like you in my life, always know what to do to make me feel better."

Anita laughed. As usual, Kika hardly lets her get a word in.

"And you look gorgeous, by the way. I am still working off of this morning's makeup," Kika began to fan her face with her hands.

Anita laughed again, "you look, lovely girl," she loved Kika so much, her fun and loving personality really encouraged others. But Anita was now about to mellow the mood. She needed Kika's advice on this mysterious phone call that Nati had.

"Sit down Kika, I need to pick your brain on something," Anita said in a serious tone.

Kika sat down quickly. She knew something was wrong as Anita's eyes slowly started to well up.

"Last night at about two in the morning, I heard Nati on the phone to someone I believe was another woman."

Kika's eyes widened in shock, "Are you sure?"

Anita nodded.

"What was he saying?" Kika asked.

"I could not gauge much from their conversation. He was telling her that it was late, he is with his wife, and he will call her back today. He was also apologising for something." Her voice began to choke up, and tears started to flow down Anita's cheeks.

Kika did believe that this was indeed strange behaviour from Nati. She had always found him incredibly controlling and, in a way, felt Anita had lost herself being with him. But he was not a bad person and had always been incredibly loving to her friend.

"I know this doesn't look great, but it doesn't look so bad either. Whoever he was talking to knows he has a wife, plus Nati absolutely adores you. He will never ever hurt you." Kika comforted.

"Do you think I should ask him about the conversation? I just do not want it to come across like I was spying on him." Anita asked nervously playing with her straw in her cocktail.

"Hmm." Kika thought to herself, "personally, I do not think you should. You and Nati have a great relationship, you don't want to spoil it, plus you have a baby on the way, you can't stress yourself."

"So, what should I do?" Anita asked helplessly.

Kika knew that she did not have all the answers; she was still trying to sort out her own messy dating life. "I think you should check his phone and find out who he has been speaking to, if he is meeting this person, let's follow him," Kika said imitating a spy holding a gun.

"But Kika, I thought you specifically told me that you do not want me to be stressed, I am telling you now that that plan sounds incredibly stressful."

Kika laughed, "don't worry Anita, I will be with you every step of the way, and if you do not find anything, you would know there was never anything to worry about, and you can then ask him without thinking something dishonest is taking place."

Kika

Kika got home to her flat and sat down on her living room sofa. She was still surprised that Anita was questioning Nati. Nati had always seemed like a good guy to her, and it was shocking that he would do something that would make her doubt him. The only flaw she could see in their relationship was how Anita had lost her spirit and drive. When they were younger, Anita was not only smart and had a lot going for her, she also loved to sing. But now, Kika could not even remember the last time she heard Anita break into a song. It was as if she had lost a piece of herself.

Kika's thoughts were disrupted by her phone ringing - it was her mother requesting to FaceTime.

"Good evening, mummy," Kika said, smiling. She had missed her parents' counsel ever since they had moved to Abuja, the capital city of Nigeria.

"Kika, my darling, I miss you, o. Your father is here too," Mrs Taiwo, her mother said.

"My baby Kiks, what's up now? Are you coming from church?" Her father asked, chiming into the screen.

Kika laughed. Being an only child, she and her parents were very close. Kika was grateful for how much they invested in her. She was treated like an absolute queen by her father and loved so dearly by her mother.

"No, daddy, I met up with Anita after work to catch up."

"Oh, Anita, how is she doing? Aisha told me she is expecting - we give God all the glory," Mrs Taiwo said. She was very close to Anita's mother.

"Yes, she is expecting. I am so happy for her," Kika continued bracing herself for what she knew her mother would say next.

"Lord! When would it be my turn, o?" She started wailing on the phone, lifting her hands into the air.

Kika rolled her eyes. She knew her mother desperately wanted her to move on with her life. She felt that even if she was not married, at least she should have a boyfriend, something to show she was thinking about it. However,

Kika was helpless. It was not like she was not open and trying to meet someone. Just the other night, she went on a date with a real potential - Femi, unfortunately, that did not work out.

"Mummy, I am trying - it is just not yet my time," Kika said, trying to console her mother, who was looking down at the floor. Her father was rubbing her back, trying to comfort her before he looked back up at Kika and mouthed, "don't worry about it."

Kika loved her father for this. He was the less dramatic of the two and believed in God's timing. He never put any pressure on her to marry as he understood that marriage is not a joke, and it was necessary to marry right.

"Mummy," Kika said, exasperated. "Trust me when I tell you that I am praying, and I am hoping to meet someone. All I ask is that you believe also."

Mrs. Taiwo looked at Kika with tears in her eyes. "Okay love, as long as you are not too comfortable. Time is going."

Kika was beyond irritated. Why did her mother blame her for her 'single' status? She was going to be 30 in a couple of years, and everyone around her was getting married. So, there was a lot of pressure that she did feel from society. But her mother made it seem that she is purposely trying to remain single.

Kika said goodbye to her parents and headed to the kitchen to make herself some tea. The call weighed heavily on her mind. Is there something wrong with her?

She put her all into work, and her boss treated her like she was disposable every single day. She was open to dating and meeting someone, and no one seemed to show any interest. Kika could not understand why this was all happening to someone who is a believer. She believed in

God more than all her friends combined. Why was she not progressing in life like the others?

Kika hated feeling like this. Comparing herself to others was something she deeply struggled with growing up, but she thought that she had overcome that. Why had she come back to this place?

She took the tea she had made, headed back to the living room, and sat on the sofa. The conversation she just had, made her question herself. She opened up a box that was under the side table. The box was filled with past journals she had written over the years. She began to rummage through it to try to locate a particular journal she had written in the past about purpose and God's plan for her life. After looking for about ten minutes, she eventually found the journal, which she had written in, 18 months prior. As she flipped through the pages, she came across a scripture:

Habakkuk 2:3 'For the vision is yet for the appointed time; It hastens toward the goal, and it will not fail. Though it tarries, wait for it; for it will certainly come, it will not delay'.

Kika read through what she had written about the passage. She was reminded of how God's timing was important, how her desires will come to pass and it will be worth the wait. She smiled. It was incredible how the Bible had answers to everything she struggled with - it just encouraged her.

She continued to flick through the pages, reminiscing about other struggles she had had in the past.

"I'm sure the right person is coming - it just is not yet my appointed time," she said to herself.

She looked at how messy the floor of the living room looked. She found that she always had to rearrange the room every single time she wanted to see scriptures based on a topic.

"It would be amazing if I could have just gotten this straight away without messing up the whole living room." She said to herself sarcastically as she dragged herself off the sofa to the floor. She began to neatly pile up all her journals and place them into the box. At that moment, one of the sheets from a journal from about three years ago flew out. All that was on the page, was a single scripture.

Jeremiah 29:11 'For I know the plans I have for you,' declares the Lord, 'plans to prosper you and not to harm you, plans to give you hope and a future.'

The verse touched her heart. God's plan will give her hope and a future - so why should she worry about anything? She continued to stare at the verse, and an idea suddenly came to mind.

"Cards of Courage," she said to herself as she wrote it down in her current journal. Kika was very creative and very good with words. She thought of creating a pack of 50 cards, each one about a particular topic. "Purpose," she whispered, "I could design them, make them pretty and easily portable." She thought about all her friends who have struggled with different issues. Anita was not interested in Christianity at all, and Tara and Mimi were neither here nor there. Kika felt that these cards could make an impact. She thought it was a fantastic idea.

She hurried into her study with her journal and Bible to pray about the idea. As she prayed, she continued to get more and more ideas and more and more scriptures. She wrote them down in her journal one by one. She opened her laptop and began to create the 'Cards of Courage', adding vibrant colours and creative fonts.

"These look so cool," she said to herself, "and it's about to change everyone's lives." She said, smiling.

At that moment, a text message came through from Anita.

A journal to the reader

Dear Reader,

In the previous journal, we discussed how we need to take the spotlight off ourselves and focus on other people. I really admire how, in this chapter, some of the ladies did just that in their encounters.

Anita noticed how Mimi had covered up a black eye and took time out of her day to check up on her even as she had a slight intuition that Mimi was being dishonest about something.

Kika could sense something was bothering Anita when she got a call from her while she was at work. But even though she could not talk at that moment, she suggested they met up later.

It is not like these two didn't have anything going on in their lives. Anita is pregnant and in a very happy place in her life, while Kika was still going back and forth with her own pressures with work and dating. But both of them took time out of their busy schedules to focus on their friends, who they believed were hurting.

Be your brother or sister's keeper, be there for them as you have no idea what they may be going through.

Philippians 2: 4 "Let each of you look not only to his own interests, but also to the interests of others."

I remember a few years ago I was at a friend's house party. It was so much fun, as you can imagine. A lot of people were there. There was good music, food, and drinks - we were having a good time. During the evening, I was talking to the host (my friend) about something, and she responded graciously, smiling, and even made a joke. On the outside, she seemed fine, but I could somehow sense that she was burdened in some way. So, I asked her if she was okay, and she looked at me in absolute shock. "How did you know?" She said to me as she thought she was hiding it quite well. It turns out her boyfriend had broken up with her that morning, but because she had already planned this party, she needed to bury her emotions to get through the evening.

If I were too busy having fun and fully concentrated on the party and myself, I would not have taken a moment to look at my friend and notice that she was actually in pain.

I think it is important to be in touch with the Holy Spirit so that He can give you the word of knowledge on others. Sometimes it is just about being still.

Journal Task 4: Reach out to people close to you and spend time nurturing those friendships. As I said in the previous journal, there is a reason they are in your life, so try to ensure that you get to know them deeply and not just at surface level. As you spend quality time with these people, pray for them, and try and listen to what God says about the situation. Be in touch with the Holy Spirit.

Tip: To help you develop a relationship with the Holy Spirit, spend time getting to know Him like you get to know your friends. Read about Him, pray to Him, worship Him, and listen. You will be surprised at how He will begin to speak to you, and you will start to hear from Him.

Lots of Love X

Simi Alexis Romeo

CHAPTER FIVE

Anita

That evening when Nati went to take his usual long shower before bed, Anita thought it was the perfect opportunity to begin her investigation and look into Nati's phone. Throughout their whole relationship, she had never attempted or felt the need to search through any of Nati's private information. She was devastated that this now appears to be her reality. "If I find nothing, I don't know if I can live with the guilt of not trusting him," Anita whispered to herself. She walked to his side of the bed and picked up his phone, which he had put on charge. She tapped the screen, and the phone lit up, asking for the passcode.

"Passcode, oh my goodness, what can the passcode be?" She thought to herself. She typed Nati's birthday digits, "no, that's not right," she put her birthday digits in - '03-04-90'. Anita's face lit up. She could not believe it had actually worked. She also felt quite giddy to find that her birthday was her husband's passcode.

At this point, she felt even more guilt that she was snooping and being a distrustful wife, but she knew she needed to know. She went to the WhatsApp app and started scrolling through his recent chats. She got to the end, and there were no unfamiliar names. She gave a sigh of relief, "I'm sure the conversation was nothing."

She sent a message to Kika,

[I just went through his WhatsApp messages - All Okay! Thanks love X]

She laid back on her bed and started thinking of her and Nati's relationship. How good he had always been to her. He definitely doesn't deserve an insecure wife who doesn't trust him.

A loud vibration disrupted her thoughts. Kika had responded.

[That's good to hear hun. Did you find out who he was talking to at 2 am?]

Anita rolled her eyes, how could she be so slow, that was the first thing she should have checked. She picked up Nati's phone, put in the passcode once again, and went straight to his call log. Nati had made several calls relating to business that day, which made Anita almost miss the random call at 2 am in the midst of other random calls. "But this doesn't tell me anything," she thought to herself.

At that moment, a message came through on Nati's WhatsApp. It was the same number that he had spoken to last night and she did not want to open it. Even though she knew that this message could be the answer to her worries, she was anxious it might be something she would be better off not seeing. Either way, her guts were telling her she must.

[Hey Nati, I know you told me not to WhatsApp you, but you aren't returning any of my calls. Look, I know this baby has come as a shock to you, but you can't neglect your duties. Please give me a call, asap!]

Anita's heart almost exploded - who is Nati ignoring? Is this person referring to her baby, or is it another baby this person is talking about? What duty is Nati supposedly neglecting?

Anita opened the message and realised that Nati had archived this person's messages. She scrolled up and quickly read through all of them. Her name was D. She and Nati had been sending each other flirtatious messages for two years. Anita's heart stopped when she came across one message in particular.

[So, I think spending time in London together two months ago can never be forgotten.]

[Why not?] Nati replied.

[Because... I'm pregnant, and the baby is yours.]

Anita dropped Nati's phone and collapsed just as Nati was coming out of the shower.

"Anita, Anita!" He screamed, "Are you okay?"

She started to bleed.

Nati was too much in a panic to notice that Anita had been with his phone. He quickly summoned the driver, then called out to his mother, who happened to be visiting. They all quickly got ready and made their way to the hospital with Anita.

"I'm so sorry. Unfortunately, we were unable to find a heartbeat." The doctor said to Nati.

Silence overwhelmed the room.

"Your wife, however, has woken up and is doing better, we will be able to discharge her later today."

The doctor's voice was chilling; the couple have lost the

baby they had been expecting for years. Nati was devastated, but for now, he was more worried about his wife. How was she going to cope, and what exactly caused her to collapse?

Nati sighed, "Thank you, doc." He had to be somewhat grateful, at least his wife was alive.

He slowly opened the hospital room door, trying not to startle his wife - the door screeched. Anita was lying down on the bed facing the window. She had her back to the door. The lights had been dimmed, and all Nati could see was the back of Anita's head and the shadow of her body falling across the hospital floor. The room was silent, but the atmosphere was thick with tension.

Nati stood there for a brief moment before finally summoning the courage to speak.

"Anita baby, are you okay?" he said in a low tone.

"Nati, I have lost our baby. I guess me becoming a mother is just not meant to be. Please apologise to your mother, I cannot face her right now," wept Anita.

"Babe, you do not need to be sorry, there will be plenty more to come, I'm just happy that you are okay and alive. You are all I care about."

Anita turned to face her husband. "Oh, yes, of course, there will be plenty to come," Anita said aggressively, "for you anyway."

Nati looked at her confused, "What do you mean?"

She could not believe that Nati would disrespect her so much that he would have an affair, impregnate another woman and not even have the decency to tell her. Now she has lost her baby due to the shock of it all. Before Anita could attempt to respond, his mother walked into the room.

"Osinachi, I came out of the bathroom, and the doctor refuses to give me any information. He said you guys are ready to be discharged, please how is my grandchild?"

"Anita is doing well," Nati said awkwardly, giving his mother 'the eye', trying to remind her that his wife had just suffered a traumatic episode. "Unfortunately, the baby did not make it."

"Ahhhhh," Nati's mother screamed and fell to the floor. "My grandchild, o!" She lifted her head to the ceiling and began to yell, "God, why, why did you give my son a wife that is unable to bear a child?"

"MUM!"

"Its true Nati. I told you not to go for these spoilt girls, they have spoiled themselves while they were young, and now they can't even have children - what is your purpose of being a woman, Anita?"

Anita boiled with anger. She had always tried to be the bigger person with Nati's mother. She was always respectful and allowed her to dig at her time and time again, but this time, she was not having it.

"Mummy, don't worry, you will be a grandmother very soon, and I'm sure you will be happy to know that I will not be the mother!" Anita said sternly.

Nati and his mother looked at Anita in bewilderment.

"Yes! Did you not know that Nati is expecting a child?"

Nati and his mother gasped.

"Yes, I saw the messages between you and Miss D, and I know you're expecting a baby with her. So, you, your mother and Miss D – oh, and her gorgeous grandchild can live happily ever after," Anita said with attitude.

She lifted the duvet cover and sat at the edge of her hospital bed as she put on her white designer trainers.

Nati hesitated to speak, baffled at how Anita could have seen the messages.

His mother looked at her son in disappointment, before

she insensitively realised she will still become a grand-mother anyway. She smirked, turned around, and left the room. She will ask Nati about her grandchild at a more appropriate time, she thought to herself.

"Anita, where are you going? You can't just leave on your own," Nati exclaimed.

"Oh, so now you care about my well-being?" She questioned, "Nati, I just lost our baby that we had been waiting for, for so long, and my 'faithful' husband on the same day. I think we are done here. Kika is coming to pick me up, and I am going to stay with her for some time, I need space."

"But you haven't lost me, I am still here, and I still want to be with you?"

"Are you kidding me? Do you actually think I want to be with you right now? We are done here!" She stormed out of the hospital room, trying to mask the pain she was feeling in her lower abdomen.

He tried to stop her to explain, but he could not find the appropriate words to calm the situation. He had ruined and broken an amazing relationship with his wife. There was nothing he could really say that could make Anita trust him or feel any better. He knew he had spoilt something special, and their lives were about to change forever.

Mimi

"What would you like to drink, my dear?" Asked Mrs Coker, Mimi's mother.

"Just some cold water with ice, please, mummy."

Mimi's mother carefully brought over a tray with two clean glasses and an ice bucket.

"Thank you, mummy," Mimi said, smiling at her.

"So, to what do I owe this visit, you did not even bring my boys?" Mrs Coker said while imitating rocking a baby.

"Yes, I didn't." Mimi hesitated and looked over at her mum. She honestly knew that what she was about to tell her about Rayo will break her heart, and she really did not want to do that. She also wanted to tell her at a time when she knew Rayo would be in meetings all day and that her father was not at home. Knowing him, he will just head over to Rayo and most likely make the situation worse.

"Demilade, please take off your sunglasses - it is very rude to wear them indoors," said Mrs Coker. Mimi had tried her best to disguise the cuts and bruises all over her face. She had allowed her big hair to cover as much of her face as possible, she wore large sunglasses to hide her bruised eye, and she topped it all by wearing bright red lipstick to mask the blisters on her lips.

"Mum, I need to tell you something, but whatever I tell you, you have to promise not to overreact as it can cost me my life, my babies' lives, and potentially your life, too." Mimi said sternly.

Mrs Coker sat up closer to Mimi. She knew her daughter - oh, so very well, and she had recently been feeling very uncomfortable about her marriage. For Mrs Coker, Mimi did not have to say anything. She reached her hand towards Mimi's face and gently removed her sunglasses and tucked her hair behind her ears.

Then, she gasped. Mimi had a swollen eye and cuts all over her face. Beneath the red lipstick, she could see the busted lip. Mrs Coker's heart sank, and she began to well up as she continued to inspect her daughter's face. She was trying her best to hold it in to avoid Mimi seeing, but Mimi could see the pain in her mother's eyes. Tears began to flow. Both ladies sat on the sofa, hugging and weeping.

"We need to get you out of there," Mrs Coker finally said.

"Yes, mum, but how? He will come after me, the boys, maybe even you - I cannot risk that."

"Never mind me, we need to protect you from him. I cannot lose you, Demilade."

"Mummy!" Mimi pleaded, "Please act out of wisdom and not emotion. Do not let this ruin our lives."

"I won't, but how long has this been going on for?" Mrs Coker questioned.

"Pretty much our whole marriage - it was verbal abuse until I gave birth to the boys, then it became physical."

"Why are you just telling me?" Mrs Coker said worriedly.

"I felt I could handle the verbal abuse; I felt I was a strong cookie. Plus, I had fought the world to marry this man - I did not feel it was enough to leave. By the time it turned physical, he was threatening my life, your life, the twins' lives, and I was too scared."

"Oh darling," Mrs Coker rubbed Mimi's back to show her comfort.

"Oh, and did I mention, he forces me to give him every single penny I make which he gambles with. If I do not, he beats the hell out of me."

"What?!" Mrs Coker said, stunned, covering her mouth with both hands.

"He also takes money from some of my friends' husbands and gambles with that too - most of the time, he loses the money and uses my money to pay them back," Mimi continued.

"Well, do you tell your friends this?" Mrs Coker asked.

"Of course, not mum, he will burn me alive. This beating was because Anita told me that Rayo was meeting with her husband for a big deal, and she asked my thoughts - I said nothing, but Anita used her intuition to work out that something may be amiss and told Nati not to sign the deal. He came home and beat me up because he thought I had said something to her."

"Mimi, this is devastating. If I let you go back into that house, I most definitely would have failed as a mother."

Mimi looked at her mum. She was right. Her mother would never let her go back, and to be honest, she did not want to go back either.

"But the boys are still there, mum," Mimi said, "I would have failed as a mother if I leave them in the hands of such a dangerous person."

Mrs Coker realised this was not an easy fix, and this required a lot of strategising, with prayer. "Why don't we go there together and pick up the boys?"

"Mummy, what are you not understanding? Do you think he is going to let me do that?" At this point, Mimi was extremely stressed over the whole situation - she knew her mother was trying to help, but at the same time, she knew she couldn't.

"Well, should we get the police involved - maybe just show up at the house and arrest him straight away?"

"Yes, that was the first exit plan I thought of, but what if he is let out on bail and returns to kill me?"

Mrs Coker soon became fed up with this going back and forth. "Well Mimi we need to do something." She said exasperated, "should I tell your father and brother, they may have an idea on how to go about it."

"No! No! No mummy, please do not tell them." Mimi exclaimed. Her brother was married and lived in America with his wife and daughter, and she would rather not bother him. Mimi's father was building a church in India and planned to be there for the next nine months.

"Okay, well why don't we just go to your house and get

the boys and come back - we can call the nannies ahead before we get there. How about we say a word of prayer before we go? God answers prayers, you know."

Reluctantly Mimi agreed. "Yes, okay, let's do it, but please mummy, let's not make the prayer unnecessarily long," she said, knowing how cheeky she was being.

"I will be straight to the point," Mrs Coker held Mimi's hands and bent her head down. Mimi followed suit. "Father Lord, we thank you for our lives, we thank you that we are here together. You understand this situation with Mimi and Rayo's marriage. Please protect us, give us wisdom and a way to get out of this situation. In Jesus' name, we pray."

"Amen," they both said.

At that moment, Mimi's phone began to ring. To her surprise, it was Grace, one of her nannies. Grace never called unless there was a huge emergency, and when Mimi saw her name on her phone, she began to panic.

"Grace, is everything okay with the boys - what's the problem?" Mimi asked.

"Hello Ma, the boys are fine - but the police are here, they told me to call you."

"What, about what?" Mimi asked, confused, "Have you spoken to Mr Abraham?"

"No, I haven't ma, I think that is who they are looking for," Grace replied.

Mimi was incredibly confused, why were the police looking for Rayo, was it about the abuse, or has he been caught in a fraud. Is he safe? Is he alive? "Okay, I am on my way now; see you in 20 minutes," she said.

"Mum, we need to go now; something has happened," Mimi called out to Mrs Coker.

"I will grab my bag."

Tara

While Dabira was FaceTiming her mother in her room, Tara went into the study to have a catch up with Bode. She was yet to tell him about the awkward phone call she had with Pastor Lade over the weekend. As soon as she walked in, she saw Bode on the phone, looking extremely distressed.

"Is everything okay, babe?" she whispered, trying her best not to interrupt.

He nodded nervously and put his finger out to signify to Tara to wait.

"What do you mean you cannot find him?!" Bode yelled. "You mean he has run away with - and there is nothing you can do about it?"

Tara started feeling extremely anxious, Bode had gotten angry in the past, but this was the first time she had seen him looking almost scared. She gently placed her hand on his back and could feel the sweat coming through his shirt.

"What's going on, Bode?" she whispered.

He looked at Tara with sorrow in his eyes and mouthed to her, "we are finished."

Tara began to wonder what Bode meant by 'we are finished'. She racked her brain about whether or not they had done anything wrong or out of the ordinary. She nervously stood back at the door and watched Bode walk up and down his office, alternately shouting, begging, and screaming at this person on the phone.

As soon as he got off the call, he sat back in his office chair, staring at the floor. He then let out a big sigh, folded his arms across the desk, and buried his head in it.

"Bode, what's going on? I am scared." Tara said, gently walking towards her fiancé. As she got closer, she could see

Bode shaking. She put her arm around him, and he began to weep. For as long as Tara had known Bode, she had never seen this side to him. She could not express the worry she had.

She bent down to be level with her fiancé. "Bode, what is going on? No matter what it is, I have your back."

Bode looked up at Tara with tears in his eyes and said, "we have lost everything, Tara."

"What are you talking about?"

"The 2 Billion Naira investment we gave to Rayo - he has run away with everything. No one knows where he is."

Tara's heart sank, "What?! Are you referring to Rayo, Mimi's husband?" She whispered.

"Yes, which other Rayo do you know?" Bode said, closing his eyes tightly, hoping he could wake up from this horrific dream. "He met up with Nati and I, to tell us about this amazing deal - too good to be true. Nati luckily pulled out last minute."

This was not the first time Bode had invested in a business idea that Rayo had pitched to him and his company, but this was the first time it had been such a huge, life-changing amount. Rayo had proposed a scheme to build a housing estate powered by renewable energy, and Bode thought this was definitely something he needed to get involved in. He did not only like the idea, but he also readily trusted Rayo, whom he met through Tara, being the husband to one of her best friends, Mimi.

"So where did he go, have you tried to speak to Mimi?" Tara asked

"Yes, I have called her, but she is not picking any of my calls," Bode said, exasperated. "My lawyer said the police have been in touch with her, and apparently she has no idea where he is."

Tara was dumbfounded. Did Mimi know what Rayo

was up to? She had always found him weird, especially because Rayo was first an actor with no qualifications, met Mimi, and became a businessman. They had been married for two years with twin boys, but every time they went to visit them, Rayo would always be concerned about what Bode was wearing and trying to convince Bode to go into business with him.

After a while, Bode began to test the waters by investing small amounts - between N500K and N5 million - in Rayo's deals. Rayo would always return double or triple the amount, sometimes even ahead of the due dates. No wonder Bode felt he could trust him with N2 billion after years of profitable returns. But what did this all mean for them?

She gently rubbed Bode's back. "Babe, this is a mess. That amount of money cannot just disappear," Tara continued to rub Bode's back nervously. "I am positive that no matter the outcome, we are going to be alright, I believe in you." Tara was saying all the right things she felt she could say. In reality, she was freaking out. Knowing that she desires to throw the wedding of the century and start a top business, the thought of losing so much money frightened her.

"So, do we have no money at all?" She asked, nervous about how he might react.

"No, thank God. I invested about 200 million Naira in several other places, but that is all I have Tara, we honestly need to cut back on everything until I get this all ironed out," Bode said sternly.

Tara was grateful that there was still some money in the bank, but she heard Bode loud and clear. 'Cut back?' She dreaded ever having to do that.

"Sorry, I need to take this phone call; it's my lawyer, let's be hopeful." Bode began to speak on the phone as

Tara left his office. She could not believe her best friend's husband got her and Bode into this mess. She had heard about people getting drawn into fraudulent scams, but she never thought that would ever be her story. It seemed like something from the movies.

But why would you trust one person with so much money? She, however, was not going to question Bode. For a 32-year-old man, he had done pretty well for himself and achieved a lot. In her mind, if he was able to make 2 billion Naira before, he could make it again.

She picked up her phone to give Mimi a call. She knew Mimi could not have had anything to do with this; she's got too much to lose. Her event company had been doing amazingly well, and a lot of people trusted her. She would not have embarked on anything that will jeopardise it all.

"Hello," a shaken Mimi answered the call.

"Mimi, hey! Are you okay?" Tara asked, surprised she picked up the phone.

"Tara, I am so sorry he did this to you, this madman has stolen over N5 billion from my clients and friends, I am so embarrassed, and I promise I had nothing to do with it. You have to believe me."

Tara could hear the trembling in Mimi's voice. "Don't worry, Mims. I know you had nothing to do with it. I am sure they will find him."

"Thanks, Tara, I am so sorry - please tell Bode too," she wept as she hung up the phone.

Tara was recovering from the shock of emotion from the phone call when she saw her cousin Dabira walking in the hallway.

"Hey Tara, I have been looking everywhere for you, Mum said I should greet -," she noticed that Tara seemed a bit jittery. "Are you okay?"

"Yes, I am fine, Bode and I, just need to sort some things

out." There was no way Tara was going to let her cousin know what had just occurred. Partly because it was a private issue between her and Bode, they needed to understand the impact of what had happened before bringing in third parties. But also, because she did not want anyone to know they were now not as wealthy as they once were. "So, we are going for drinks on Friday, with my best friends, Anita and Kika," she said awkwardly, trying to change the subject.

"Oh, I am so excited to meet your friends that you speak so highly of." Dabira paused, "what about Mimi?"

"Well, Mimi can't make it," Tara said, awkwardly. Although she was yet to invite her friends, she knew she wasn't ready to face Mimi."

"Oh well, maybe next time! So, what is on the wedding agenda?" Dabira asked excitedly. Ever since Tara got engaged to Bode, she had wanted to get involved in the planning of her "big sister's" wedding. "Have we picked a date yet?"

"Yes. So, we are thinking March next year, here in Lagos," Tara said, smiling.

"What, you mean ten months from now? That's pretty soon, Tara."

"Well, Bode and I have been pretty much inseparable for a few years now, and have been engaged for a couple of months. If we got married tomorrow, it still wouldn't feel like it's too soon." Tara assured her.

Dabira was not so sure, "Look, I am not only thinking about the fact that it may be too soon for you guys as a couple but listen, the whole of your family are currently living in the UK and ten months is not enough time for everyone to get everything together and prepare for the wedding."

"Hmm, yes, I do see your point. How long do you

think I should give it?" Tara said while nervously playing with her fingernails. Pushing the wedding back due to her family needing time to be a part of it was a believable reason. She'd rather everyone think that than think she had no money to pay for it.

"I would say at least 18 months from now - it will also give you and Bode time to get everything together financially."

Tara was taken aback by Dabira's comment. "What do you mean? Bode and I can more than happily afford the wedding - we do not even need time."

"I know Tara, but more money is always better, right? I did not mean anything by that, sorry." Dabira was reminded how defensive Tara could be. "So how's the fashion label?" she said, changing the subject.

"Well, Bode and I were discussing this. I have pretty much completed the collection. I have just a few more tweaks. Wait here, let me show you." Tara ran to her bedroom to bring out the collection she had made. "At the moment, they are just samples, but what do you think?" She said, laying them out one by one on the sofa.

Dabira slowly began to work through the collection studying the details and noting the creativity.

"Wow, Tara, these are impressive, look at the detailing. You have really outdone yourself," Dabira said, dazzled by the collection.

"Thanks so much," Tara giggled.

"So what's next, have you found a buyer yet?"

"So, I was thinking of launching it myself as my own brand - 'The Tara Cole Collection'." Tara stared into the distance, gently waving both of her hands from side to side.

Dabira laughed, "that is excellent, sis!"

"I was going to ask you whether you will be interested in modelling them for me?" Tara asked.

Dabira looked shocked at Tara, the last time she had done any modelling was when she was twenty-one, six years ago, and she hated the pictures so much, she had sworn she would never do it again.

"Tara, you know how I feel about modelling, it is a bit awkward for me."

"Oh, please, you are slim, tall, and beautiful. Plus, you are not going to have that fantastic body forever. Do this for me please, Dabira? Bode thinks it will cut down on costs, and with the wedding I want to have -," she stopped, realising she had portrayed that she and Bode are struggling with finances.

Dabira thought about the comment Tara made about her body; she was right; she was not getting any younger or any skinnier. "You know what, only for you sis, let's model 'The Tara Cole Collection'!" Dabira said, gesturing the hand movements.

"You will do that for me, Dabira?" Tara smiled.

"Absolutely! Why not?"

A journal to the reader

Dear Reader,

Have you ever felt your life was going at a steady pace, and you were happy and at peace, then suddenly, things take a turn for the worse?

It was only a few chapters ago that Anita felt her struggles of not being able to have children had come to an end. Now she has not only gone back to that place with her miscarriage, but she has also found out that her husband has been unfaithful and is having a baby with another woman.

The same thing with Tara, she was happy, planning her wedding and looking forward to her new fabulous and wealthy life with Bode, and now she appears to have lost nearly everything.

I think people must understand and realise whether you are Christian or not that life is a journey, and on that journey, there will be smooth roads and bumpy roads.

It would help if you were prepared because everyone will have to go through them.

How do you keep prepared?

With the armour of God! (Ephesians 6:11)

When you get to the bumpy road in life, you need God's word to help you get through.

Psalm 18:39 "You armed me with strength for battle; you humbled my adversaries before me."

Psalm 27:1 "The LORD is my light and my salvation - whom shall I fear? The LORD is the stronghold of my life - of whom shall I be afraid?"

Joshua 1:9 "Have I not commanded you? Be strong and courageous! Do not tremble or be dismayed, for the Lord your God is with you wherever you go."

These scriptures and many others in the Bible will give you peace and comfort in times of trouble.

If you are currently on a bumpy road, here are some ways to get through it.

1. Always remember that God is in control.

The 2020 global pandemic was one of the hardest moments of my life. I went through a breakup, I was anxious about my role at work, I suffered from multiple panic attacks over the safety of my loved ones, and I was alone dealing with all this the whole time. What helped me was remembering that God's hand was on my life, and all things work together for my good. (Romans 8:28). I know it seems easier said than done, but saying it out loud every day helped me. Try and look for what God is trying to teach you in these tough times. It will encourage you and remind you that he does have a plan, and it is all for a purpose.

2. Remember the good things God has done for you.

Sometimes we easily forget that God has actually helped us out in so many ways before. What makes this way any different? By going back and revisiting these, you are reminded of his faithfulness.

3. Being aware of what brings you joy.

I noticed for me that during this bumpy road in my life, I found it hard to pray. So, I found that listening to worship music, going for long walks, doing yoga, and picking up new skills really helped me. Find out what helps you.

4. Speak to loved ones.

Talk to those that you trust to help you during this time. It is important to note that just because a person is your friend does not mean they are equipped to help in this particular situation, and that, in turn, does not make them a bad friend. God will bring the right person to you who may have gone through something similar or are gifted in that particular area.

5. Thank God.

Have faith that it will soon be over, and there is light at the end of the tunnel.

Journal Task 5: Write down the situations you are struggling with at the moment and say the following prayer:

'Dear God, I hand over to you my current situation. I understand you know the end from the beginning, and therefore I will get through this bumpy road. Take the wheel in this situation in Jesus' name. Amen'

Tip: If you don't prepare to handle things, our emotions tends to handle us.

Lots of Love X

Simi Alexis Romeo

CHAPTER SIX

Kika

"Look at what I've been working on," Kika said excitedly, bringing her 'Cards of Courage' out of her bag to show Daisy.

Although Anita had been living with Kika after the turmoil she went through with Nati, Daisy was the first person Kika chose to show her cards to. Daisy was a Christian, and Kika felt she would understand the value of them.

"What is it?" Daisy asked confused, looking at the cards Kika had handed to her.

"So, they are words of affirmation cards. It has scriptures and quotes, all to do with the topic, 'Purpose'. I am thinking of putting together a collection with different topics," Kika said, smiling through the awkwardness. She felt Daisy did not seem too keen on them, "I designed them myself."

"I can tell," Daisy said giggling. "They look like kids made them."

Kika looked at Daisy in shock; she was not expecting that reaction from her. Daisy had always been quite supportive when it came to her journalism work. So, this reaction made her question what she'd created.

"Well, I guess you do not like the design - but I think the idea is great, and it will have such a positive effect on those going through hard times. One of my friends is staying with me, and she is going through a tough time. I think I am going to leave these cards with her," Kika said, now even more convinced of the benefits of the concept.

"Oh yeah, I think that's a good idea. Is your friend a Christian?"

Before she could even respond, Ms Gozy walked into the open office area.

"Kika, you are quite close to Mimi Coker, right?"

"Yes, she is one of my best friends. She is Mimi Abraham now," Kika said cheekily. She was confused as to why Ms Gozy had brought Mimi's name up.

"Well, I don't know if your 'best friend' has updated you about her fraudulent husband," Ms Gozy said, loving every moment of sharing this gossip.

"What, no? What has happened?" Kika asked worriedly. She had always known that Rayo was such a weird individual, and she had never felt peace about him.

"Her husband has stolen as much as 5 Billion Naira from a number of Mimi's friends and clients, my dear - it is all coming to light now." Ms Gozy could not stop smiling. Kika had never seen her in such a chuffed mood, and she was confused as to why. "All the magazines and media companies are thrilled by this story, but 'Hello Lagos" has the inside scoop," she said dancing.

Kika began to realise that Ms Gozy was expecting her to provide information about Mimi, but she knew she could never betray her friend in such a dastardly manner.

"Hmm, Ms Gozy, I have not heard anything from Mimi, so I am afraid I do not have the 'inside scoop'," Kika said boldly.

"Oh, Kika, you have so much to learn," she said in a patronising way, "I need you to go and GET the inside scoop. Speak to Mimi and let her tell you her side of the story, then come and share it with us. Simple as." Ms Gozy was serious. Working as a pop culture journalist for so long, she had forgotten what loyalty was and wouldn't recognise it if it hit her in the face. All she cared about was making money for herself and a name for her brand.

Kika sighed, although she had no idea what Mimi was going through, there was no way she would throw her under the bus. "Ms Gozy, I am afraid I cannot do that. She is my best friend."

Ms Gozy looked at Kika unimpressed. "You see what I mean when I tell you that you are not ready to be promoted. You need to let loose and be a bit more risky." She got close to Kika and whispered in her ear, "friends come and go, but your career at 'Hello Lagos' will stay forever - so what is it going to be?"

Kika knew exactly what Ms Gozy meant by this, she was threatening her. She will lose her job if she does not get the information from Mimi. She gulped and turned her head to look into Ms Gozy's eyes. "Ms Gozy, I am sorry I can't."

Ms Gozy frowned and let out a huge sigh, before storming out of the open office area.

"Wow, that was intense," Daisy said, breaking the silence.

"I mean Daisy; it is so unfair. That is my best friend. Mimi has been there for me the many times I have had sleepless nights over this job. I will not choose to hurt her just to stay in a job where I don't even feel appreciated."

Daisy nodded. "Yes, I agree with you, but it is weird that your friend did not tell you about this."

Kika began to think. Why hadn't Mimi told her? She felt that Tara probably knows because Tara and Mimi are very close. Mimi also would have probably told Anita if Anita was not going through her own problems. Why was she always the last to know? Kika slowly began to question her friendship with Mimi just as a call came through from Ms Gozy on her iPhone.

"I'm about to be fired," she mumbled to herself as she picked up the call and went to one of the private phone booths in the office.

"Kika, I will offer you the promotion you have been asking for if you get this information for me. You can write the top stories, use your name on them, and I will double your salary to N1million a month - what do you say?"

Kika gasped. She, in no way, wanted to betray Mimi. However, Ms Gozy was giving her an offer that was out of this world. This must mean Ms Gozy was desperate for the information to offer so much.

"Ms Gozy, I would like to negotiate this offer," Kika said nervously.

"Really? Go on."

"I would like to have my own segment every single week where I discuss the concept of Purpose, and also interview people and their life journeys."

"Okay, done."

"I'm not finished," Kika said audaciously. "I would also like my salary increased to N1.5 Million, plus a 10% commission on every story I write. I will also still be given all the top stories to write with my name in the byline."

There was silence from the other end.

"Ms Gozy, are you there?" Kika asked apprehensively.

"Kika, N1.5 million is a lot. It is too much to give."

"Ms Gozy, betraying my friend is too much to give."

Kika was impressed with her newfound confidence. She could not believe she was speaking this way to her boss.

"Okay, I will do it! When can you get us the story?"

"I first need to sign a contract stating all these changes. I also need you to agree to retain me for at least a year with full pay after giving you the information." Kika was not stupid; she knew Ms Gozy could fire or demote her as soon as she gets her all the information.

Ms Gozy paused, "smart girl - you will have the new contract by the end of the week. Next week I expect the story."

Kika put down the phone in disbelief. She had just negotiated a fantastic deal for herself and was in high spirits. She looked down at the cards that Daisy had previously dismissed and read a passage that made her feel incredibly guilty.

Philippians 3:19 'Their destiny is destruction, their god is their stomach, and their glory is in their shame. Their mind is set on earthly things".

Kika remembered that she put this scripture in the 'Purpose' stack of her 'Cards of Courage' to remind her always to remain true to herself and not become greedy. She realised that betraying Mimi and being a disloyal friend were being done purely out of greed for growth for her career. It was hard because this was what Kika had been praying and waiting on the Lord for. But was it worth hurting Mimi? Was it worth her other friends being distrustful of her when she was around?

She was torn.

Mimi

Dear Mimi,

I know I have not always been the best husband to you, and I know I have caused you a lot of pain over the years. Through it all, I want you to know that I genuinely love you, and I really appreciate you for giving me a chance when no one else would. You were always so supportive of all my dreams and have gifted me with the greatest gifts of all, our sons - Daniel and Desmond.

My absconding may come as a massive shock to you, but what you are now probably hearing is true. I have taken the N5 billion and have invested it for a great future for you and the boys. You may not understand it right now, but in ten to fifteen years, you all would appreciate it.

I have gone to a place where I am positive that no one can find me. I am sorry I have had to do this to you and the boys, but you are a tough girl, and I know you can make it work.

I don't know if or when I will ever see you again, but know that I think of you guys every day, and I am looking for a way to reunite us all.

I would appreciate it if you kept this letter to yourself.
I love you, Mimi,
Rayo

As Mimi sat in the waiting room of her new lawyer's office reading the letter over and over again, she is overwhelmed with a ton of emotions. In one way, she was happy that Rayo had finally left her and her children alone. This meant that she was safe, and she did not have to worry about getting beaten or giving him any of her money ever again. On the other hand, she was angry that he had stolen money from her close friends and clients, and she was probably now responsible for the stupendous amount of debt owed to them. To top it all off, his letter to her shows how self-centred he is. How could he leave his wife and babies to deal with his mess while he goes off to live a completely new life and expect her not to show anyone the letter? Mimi was furious, hurt, and embarrassed.

"I cannot believe this. Rayo stole from my clients, stole from my family, and worst of all, from Tara and Bode," Mimi said, hugging her mother tightly. "How am I going to get out of this? Probably no one will believe that I had no part in this. I don't even have any money to pay people back - he took it all!"

Mrs Coker was at a loss for words. The whole situation will tarnish their names in Lagos society as well as severely damage their credibility. But she knew Rayo could not be less concerned with all of that.

She hid her disquiet and turned to Mimi with confidence. "Demilade, this is the time when you need to show resilience. Be bold, be strong - the Lord, your God is with you." Mrs Coker said with great conviction.

"Mum, that is easier said than done, honestly," Mimi said, tired of her mother's random callouts of bible verses.

"Mimi, I know it is easier said than done," she agreed. "But, I ask you, do you believe in the word of God?"

Mimi gave her mother a confused look - what did she mean? Of course, she did. She was brought up in the church, and her parents were both pastors. So, of course, she believed in it. "Mummy, why would you ask me that? I have been going to church my whole life."

"Yes, you have been going to church your whole life because your father and I had pretty much dragged you," she mused, "but accepting Jesus into your heart and having your own relationship with God, where you trust in His word and fully believe that He will work everything out for your good, is a whole different ball game."

Mimi thought about her mother's words. In church, when she was younger, their Sunday school teacher would always say, "Put your hand up if you haven't given your life to Christ." and every single week, Mimi would put her hands up because she loved making her way to the front of the class and receiving attention and her own special prayer. In truth, Mimi did not understand what she was doing. When she grew older, she moved to her own church and would occasionally pray, but she did not have 'the relationship' her mother speaks of.

"How do I get a relationship?" Mimi asked nervously.

"You need to seek His word, get to know God for yourself, see what He says about you and how He has moved in similar situations in the Bible. You will begin to trust Him because He is the same God yesterday, today, and forever," Mrs Coker smiled.

Mimi nodded as she listened to her mother's words. This was the first time she saw the notion of being a Christian differently.

"Good afternoon Mrs Coker and Mrs Abraham. Thank you for coming in to see us today, and I apologise for keeping you waiting. I am Angela, Mr Dare's assistant." The lady put her hand out to shake Mimi and Mrs Coker.

"Good afternoon, Is Mr Dami Dare around? I heard he had a meeting earlier on with the police regarding our situation." Mrs Coker had gotten Dami Dare, one of the best lawyers in Lagos, to handle her daughter's case. She also knew him from her church. He was one of the youth leaders, and Mrs Coker adored him.

"Yes, he is waiting in his office. Please follow me."

As the ladies walked into the office, they were greeted

by a very tall and attractive man; Mimi could not help but stare.

"Mrs Coker, it is so lovely to see you," Dami said while bowing down, showing he was brought up in a respectful African home.

"Dami, my son, how are you?" Mrs Coker asked.

"This must be your daughter you keep telling me about, Mrs Abraham," Dami said, smiling at Mimi.

Mimi could not ignore the fact that Dami was attractive. However, she was still a married woman at the end of the day and the mess she was in meant she was not open to putting the slightest energy into a relationship with any man. Her focus was getting out of this mess for the sake of herself and her sons.

"Hi, lovely to meet you, please just call me Mimi and thank you for agreeing to take on this case," Mimi said emotionally.

"No problem! Please take a seat."

Mrs Coker and Mimi sat down and made themselves comfortable. Mimi began to look around his office. Dami had received a lot of awards as a lawyer - he really was accomplished and highly recognised in the profession.

"So, I hear you received a letter?" Dami asked.

"Yes, here it is," Mimi reached into her bag to pull out the handwritten note Rayo had left her in her room and handed it to Dami. "No one has seen it except you and my mum."

Dami carefully analysed the content.

"Mimi, I would like to tell you upfront, you are not in the best place. Many of the people Rayo has hurt are rich and powerful individuals who will be desperate to get their money back and will likely do anything to do so. As you are married to Rayo, his debt is your debt. The letter and the fact you were a victim of domestic violence is good evidence, but there is still a fine line. It is going to require a lot of work."

Mrs Coker held Mimi's hands tightly, to show her support. Mimi looked nervously at her mum and back at Dami, "yes, I understand."

"All the victims have been contacted, and I would advise that as this case progresses, you and your children move out of your home to protect yourselves," Dami continued.

"Well, she will move into our house; she will be safe there." Mrs Coker said, smiling at Mimi.

"That is perfect. I assure you I will do everything in my power to make sure that we resolve this matter, and the police also are doing everything in their power to find Rayo.

"Everything will work out for good," Mrs Coker said.

"Amen!" Dami said, smiling.

A journal to the reader

Dear Reader,

If God has placed something in your heart or in you, and you were not built strongly, you may allow other people's opinions - which may not be correct - to influence you otherwise.

Kika was excited about the 'Cards of Courage' and decided to show the idea to her colleague at work, who had always been supportive of her. Daisy's reaction was hurtful to Kika. She insulted the idea, said it looked childish and dismissed it.

If Kika were not convicted and had allowed Daisy's reaction to influence her, she would probably have discarded the idea.

Meanwhile, God knows how beneficial these cards will be to her close friends and many other people.

I remember a time when people used to make fun of the fact I was quite a friendly person - I know that honestly sounds bizarre - but they used to tell me I did 'famz' which means I am overfamiliar if I said hi to someone I didn't know in a friendly manner.

At this time, I was 16 years old; so you'd think they would easily influence me, right? Well, actually, at that time, I felt they had no clue. What was wrong with being kind to others? Until one day, I met someone for the first time and said hi to them in my friendly manner, and they gave me the coldest reception ever in front of an audience of about six people. It was so embarrassing. For the next few years, I was adamant to never say hi to a person like that again. Keep it cool.

This, however, caused major problems for me. God has given me this bubbly, friendly, and approachable personality for a reason. I was beginning to come off cold and quiet to people, and I knew this was just not who God made me to be. After a while, I realised that being myself was more important than people's personal opinions of me.

Now I get compliments for being open, bubbly, and friendly.

In fact, I get chosen quite a lot to reach out to people. Isn't that amazing? What kind of Christian would I be if I was unapproachable, and people thought I was moody and had an attitude?

The message I am trying to pass on is that God's opinion matters a lot more than other people's. Human beings are fickle, so you have to do your best to take every opinion with a pinch of salt. Take it to God because he knows best.

Journal Task 6: Are there ideas that you feel God has given you that you are scared to start because of what others may say or think of you? Write these down and use this scripture to pray over it.

Deuteronomy 31:6 "Do not fear or be in dread of them, for it is the Lord your God who goes with you. He will not leave you or forsake you."

Tip: Keep God as your focus above what you see. He knows best.

Lots of Love X

Simi Alexis Romeo

CHAPTER SEVEN

Anita

It had been a week since Anita left the hospital and moved into Kika's flat. She was grieved and broken after losing her pregnancy and finding out that Nati had cheated on her and is expecting a baby from another woman. She could not process both 'losses' at once and struggled with which of the tragedies to focus on. Her mind refused to accept that her loving, devoted husband and her new miraculous baby - whom she was so looking forward to meeting, were no longer part of her.

"Why me? She whispered to herself, "I was so close to becoming a mother and running a complete household."

She aggressively jumped out of her bed and started pacing up and down the bedroom, flinging her hands in the air. "To make the situation worse, Nati did not only have an affair, but his 'mistress' also got pregnant and, it appeared she got her baby so easily without the stress and drama that I had to go through," Anita continued. "I am the wife, but it took me seven years to even fall pregnant and surprise surprise! I lose it. This life really isn't fair!" She sat down at the edge of her bed, staring into space and sighed.

"Nati's mother was right," she said to herself, "what kind of woman am I if I can't give my husband a baby - no wonder he stepped out on me."

Anita tried to hold back her tears. She felt incredibly worthless, alone, and forgotten. Any confidence she thought she had, had now departed from her. The pain Anita was feeling was deeply unfamiliar. All her life, she had grown up exceptionally popular and incredibly liked. It was one thing to have fertility issues, but being cheated on broke her. She had never been second place in her life. She had always been at the top in school, friendships, and relationships. Handling the pain of being in second place to Nati's mistress was not something she felt she was able to do.

"Why me?" Anita cried to herself. "What did I do wrong?"

Her phone started to ring - it was Nati. He had been trying to reach her ever since the ordeal at the hospital. He had been calling and messaging constantly, but Anita felt she had nothing to say to him. She felt so shattered by the betrayal that she couldn't even function properly; she could not eat or sleep and refused to leave her bedroom at Kika's house.

She reached for her phone on the bedside table and flung it across the room in anger. The phone hit the wall and smashed onto the bedroom floor. At that moment, Kika ran into the room.

"What is going on here?" Kika asked, alarmed.

Trying to catch her breath, Anita slid off her bed, laid on the floor, and continued to weep.

"Aww, Anita," Kika rushed towards her best friend and

sat next to her on the floor. She wrapped her arms around her and stroked her curly afro. Anita began to feel relaxed, rested her head on Kika's shoulder, closed her eyes, and drifted off to sleep.

A few hours passed, and then, there was a knock on the door.

Anita opened one of her eyes as the bedroom door slowly opened and closed them straight back when she saw it was Kika coming in. She wondered how she got back into bed and assumed that Kika must have moved her.

"Hey love, I brought you your favourite - fried rice and peppered chicken with a side of plantain - yummy," Kika said optimistically, carrying the tray of home-cooked food into Anita's room.

"Thanks, but I'm not hungry," Anita said without looking up at Kika.

"Anita, you have got to eat something. You have barely eaten anything since you've been here," she pleaded.

Kika's heart was breaking for Anita as Nati was all she had ever known.

"Come on, hun; I'll feed you," Kika enticed, bringing the spoon towards her mouth.

Anita quickly sat up. She was down, but not to the point where her friend would need to pity her or treat her like a child. "It's okay; I think I'm old enough to feed myself," Anita said sarcastically. "But thanks so much for taking care of me," she said while tying her hair into a bun.

Kika smiled, "That's what friends are for," she said as she placed the tray onto Anita's lap. "Speaking of friends, I think we should organise a 'girls'-night-in' with Mimi and

Tara to try and take your mind off everything. I think everyone is going through a tough time-"

"No! No! No!" Screamed Anita, "I don't want the other girls to know about this."

"But they are your friends, they care," Kika pleaded.

"No, Kika, my mother doesn't even know about this, no!"

And that was final.

Anita was not comfortable with the idea of her mother finding out about Nati and the baby. She felt she needed to understand the situation clearly before involving her mother, especially as it was likely she would try to convince her to reunite with Nati, without taking the pains to think it all through.

Aisha Fawun is a traditional African woman. She is passionately loud, opinionated, and extremely dramatic, but she is also passionate about her love for her family, which Anita admired.

Anita had seen how her father had treated her mother over the years. Although he was kind towards her and provided for the family financially, he always had many women around and was quite the 'Lothario'. Her mother turned a blind eye to it all, "gosh, these women are so desperate," she would say, or "wow, how some women can do anything for a Chanel bag."

There was a time her mother had caught her father and one of her friends having dinner together. Her father, by way of explanation, casually said he had bumped into her, and they decided to 'catch up' for a drink. However, Anita, who was with her mum at the time, had seen them touching and laughing - it was definitely a dubious situation.

Although, on the one hand, Anita saw her mother as strong, loving, and powerful, she regretfully also felt her mother was unable to stand up for herself when it came to her father's antics. This was something she always feared would happen to her, which was why she knew she could not have her mother influence her decision on whether to reunite with Nati, without properly thinking about it.

As Anita started eating the fried rice and chicken that Kika had brought up, she suddenly realised how famished she was. She proceeded to gobble up what was her favourite dish scarcely coming up for air.

"Okay, calm down, love, don't choke!" Kika laughed "Oh, and make sure you look under the plate once you're finished - I left you something," Kika said excitedly as she slowly left the bedroom.

Anita was too focused on the food to start to think of what Kika was referring to. She finished every single grain of rice and gnawed her chicken to the bone - she was fully satisfied. She looked over at the door that Kika had just left through and whispered, "thank you, bestie." She laid down and fell back into a deep sleep.

A couple of hours had passed, and Anita was slowly coming out of sleep when she heard a quiet knock, and a squeak from the door of her bedroom slowly open. She reluctantly opened her eyelids to see Kika, now all dressed up, smiling at her.

"Where are you going," she asked.

"I'm off to the mid-week service at church. You should come?" Kika said, hopeful.

"Erm, thanks, but I'll pass."

Kika looked over at Anita with some concern. Anita had never been the religious type. Her mum was a Christian, and her father was a Muslim. She always felt bewildered about her faith. As a child, her mother compelled her and her sisters to go to church every Sunday. The only thing she liked about this was playing with her friends in church, her favourite being Tara Williams. But Tara had to leave the church to move to England abruptly when her grandmother passed away. Once Tara left, church became exceptionally lonely and boring for Anita.

When it was time for her to move to England to further her education, Anita and church cut ties, and she never looked back. She also found Christianity to be very unrealistic.

"I mean, how is one person meant to follow all these rules - can't you just live your life?" She thought to herself. Being an atheist was probably the most reasonable path to follow according to her reasoning.

"Okay, dear," but know that in times of fear and anxiety, the only person that can save you is Jesus," Kika advised, putting her arms around Anita.

Anita gave Kika a dismissive hand gesture, "thanks, love, have fun."

Once Kika had left the house, Anita decided she had been moping around long enough, and it was time to get out of bed and do something productive. She opened her suitcase and buried her hands under all her clothing, before eventually coming across a journal that Kika had given her to use to monitor her pregnancy. Anita brought the journal out and started reading from the date she discovered she was pregnant. As she reminisced over her joyful emotions, tears began to fall down Anita's face once again. She took a blue pen and heavily scribbled across all the words she had written. On a fresh page, Anita began to write down a list of all the negative emotions she had felt over the past week – "hurt, pained, broken, confused, denial, mentally drained, stupid, dumb, useless, worthless, angry, sad."

On the opposite page - she wrote positive emotions she had felt.

"Blessed that I have Kika," she looked around the room, unable to think of one other thing. Frustrated, she lifted the tray with the empty plate that Kika had brought and put it on the dressing table. She was not in the mood to clean up after herself, "I'll do this later," she said to herself.

Her thoughts were interrupted when the doorbell rang. Kika was still at church, and as far as she was concerned, neither of them were expecting anybody.

She got out of bed and made her way to the front door.

"Who is it?" Anita yelled in a stern manner

"Madam, it's Innocent, Madam Kika's security guard at the front gate."

"Oh, Innocent, What is the problem?"

"Madam, a Woman is here - Mrs Fawun, she said she is your mother," yelled Innocent through the door.

"My mother?" Anita questioned in fear. What can her mother be doing here? The fact she knew she was at Kika's could only mean one thing. She must know about the whole Nati and baby situation. Her mother would be so disappointed that Anita didn't feel she could come to her.

"Okay, please let her in," Anita said, reluctantly, quickly running to the bedroom to make herself look somewhat decent. She didn't want her mother to start tearing down her appearance. She wanted to look like she was happy and that she had everything under control. This was how she lived her life - always wanting control.

She got back to the front door, just in time to open the door for her mother, who had been let in through the gate.

"Good evening mummy, this is a surprise," Anita said confidently with a counterfeit smile while hugging her.

"Anita, I have been so worried about you. You have not returned my phone calls. I had to call Nati to find out where you were. He told me everything. My baby, my heart is breaking for you," Aisha said, stroking Anita's face.

"Mummy, I'm fine. I just needed a break, away from everything," Anita said, attempting to relieve her mother of her doubts.

"I'm so hurt that you didn't tell me." This was typical of her mother, to always make things about herself. Not the fact that her daughter's life had just changed, probably forever. "You know my daughter; a woman should never leave her home. You are opening the door for the other woman to come into it and make your matrimonial home her home. You need to be careful."

This is exactly what Anita was trying to avoid. "I think I need space from that house, mummy. I need to process Nati's infidelity, his new child, his mother's attitude, and the fact I have just lost my baby," Anita listed. "Being under that roof and taking all that in, I am sure, will be detrimental to my mental health."

"Mental health?" Anita's mother laughed. "Don't be ridiculous, Anita, I thought I raised you better than this."

"What has raising me got to do with anything?" Anita thought to herself. Her blood had started to boil.

"Excuse me. I need the bathroom," Anita made an excuse just to get away from her mother at that point. She did not want to disrespect her, but she could not fathom how insensitive her mother could be.

As soon as she got into the bathroom, she bent over the sink, turned on the cold water tap, and slowly moved her hands under the running water - trying her best to calm herself down. She moved her head towards her palms and gently splashed the water on her face. She lifted her head out of the sink, reached to pick up a face towel, and carefully dabbed her face with it. She took several deep breaths and looked in the mirror.

"You got this, Anita!" she whispered to herself.

She walked out of the bathroom and back into the living room with a smile on her face.

"Is there anything I can get for you, mummy?" She asked.

"I thought you'd never ask my daughter - please can I have some green tea."

Anita smiled, "of course."

She went into the kitchen, boiled the kettle, and put a teabag into a mug. As soon as the water had boiled, she brewed the tea, put a jar of Manuka honey with a teaspoon on a tray, and took it to her mother.

"Thank you, dear," her mother said gracefully. "So, what is next? How long do you intend to stay here?"

"I'm not sure. As soon as my head is a lot clearer, I can then decide what's best for me. I am not too sure I can live with Nati, and his new child, and baby mother."

"Anita, No! You have to just suck it up. Men do all sorts; it is part of their nature. Do you know how many times your father broke our marriage vows? What matters is that you are his prized possession, and he takes care of you, which Nati does. It is your job as a wife to stand by him, for better or worse - those are the vows you made."

Anita did her best to ignore her mother's tirade, but she could not believe that her mother was owning up to her father's treachery. 'The bank of the Fawuns' and her 'loving and devoted husband' actually committed adultery? She saw this as an extremely rare moment and did her best to disguise the fact she was aware of the affairs.

"So, daddy cheated on you?" Anita asked, acting surprised.

Aisha nodded shamefully, "plenty of times."

"So were you hurt, because you masked it extremely well if you were?"

"Of course I was hurt, Anita, but I had a household to run, and I needed to protect you and your sisters from the damage of any potential fallouts resulting from those indiscretions. So, I dealt with it privately. I did not make a scene and run away," her mother said, raising her eyebrows.

"Mummy, what is with the passive-aggressive comment?" Anita was taken aback by her mother's stance. Her body became numb, and all she could feel was anger. She knew she was always brought up to have respect for her elders, which had always been easy for Anita. Why wouldn't it be? Everything had always gone the way she wanted it to go. She was a focused child who always got the best grades and made her family proud. She met Nati at the 'perfect time' and got married at the 'perfect age'. After marriage, was when the pressures of life had begun to weigh her down. Her father had passed away, she struggled with infertility, and now her marriage has fallen apart. Anita did not have the foundation to withstand pain and did not know how she was going to get through this. She also felt very betrayed by her mother, who seemed to be showing no compassion towards her.

Anita looked at her mother straight in the eye.

"Mummy!" She said sternly, "When you are done with the tea, please, you need to leave."

"Leave? Me? Who do you think you are talking to, Anita?" Aisha said, perplexed.

Anita started crying as she was disappointed with how she was speaking to her mother, but she knew she needed to protect her emotions.

"I am sorry, mum, but yes, please. Can you leave?" she said sternly.

At that second, Kika walked into the house and could immediately sense the tension. "Good evening, aunty Aisha, hello Anita, what is going on here?" Kika asked.

"I want her out now!" Anita screamed. She turned around and ran to her bedroom. She slammed the door behind her, got into her duvet, and buried her face into her pillow. This time, she refused to stop her tears; the release felt more than satisfactory. Wailing is where Anita wanted to be. She finally felt free.

Kika

Kika looked at Mrs Fawun in disbelief. Anita was not the type of person to raise her voice, especially at her mother.

"Are you okay, ma?" she said to Aisha.

"Kika, please talk to your friend. She needs to go back to her house and stop acting like a little child," Aisha said, unbothered by Anita's 'tantrum'.

Kika looked at her, confused. "Aunty, are you aware of what Nati has done? You know he has been having an affair for over a year, got this girl pregnant, and did not have the decency to tell Anita. When she found out, she was in such complete shock that she lost her baby - your grandchild?"

Aisha sighed. "Kika! Yes, I am aware. But what can we do now? We need to move on and try and have another baby."

"You want her to have children with Nati still?" Kika was in complete shock. She did not want to argue with Anita's mother, but my goodness. How could she not put her daughter's feelings before society?

"I think it is a disgrace to be married for so many years

and not have children. If Anita leaves, people will think Nati left her because Anita could not have kids and that he is now happy with a new woman who can," Aisha said concerned. "I cannot have people talking about my baby like that. Let her go back and at least get pregnant?"

Kika could not find the energy to even respond. Mrs Fawun was all about Lagos society gossip, and what people would say. Her mother had told her that Aisha Fawun was always like that from when they were both in secondary school. She cared too much about what others would think, and it stopped her from achieving so much. Kika knew there was no reasoning with her.

"Okay, aunty, I will talk to her about it," Kika said, knowing she most definitely will not.

"Thank you, my dear, please greet your mother for me," Aisha said as she left Kika's house.

Kika hurried into the guest room once Aisha had left, to check on Anita and see what she was doing.

"Are you okay, hun?" Kika said awkwardly as she entered the room.

Anita was sat on the bed with her arms wrapped around her knees, staring into space. Kika looked into Anita's eyes - they seemed almost lifeless.

"Ani, please do not take what your mother said personally. It is not her fault. Trust me - time away from Nati is what you need."

Anita looked at Kika. "I heard what she said about me going back to have a baby, Kika."

Kika nodded and released a huge sigh, "ignore her Anita, I am so proud of you. You have handled it all so well." She looked at the dressing table with the tray she left the 'Cards of Courage' on, wondering if she had looked at it at all.

"Have you finished eating?" Kika asked slyly.

"Oh yes, sorry I forgot to take my tray to the kitchen," Anita said, yawning drowsily.

"I am guessing you did not have a look at these?" Kika looked up at Anita, but she was already fast asleep. She took the cards off the tray and placed them on the dressing table. She hoped sometime soon, Anita will read the cards and hopefully feel encouraged about everything.

Kika was aware that with everything Anita was going through, in addition to the episode she just had with her mother, she needed support and encouragement more than anything.

She quietly went into her own room and began to think about her own problems. She could not believe that, in a couple of days, she would need to sign a document that will cause her to throw Mimi under the bus. She thought about calling Mimi to ask her about it, but she felt if Mimi really saw her as a good friend, then why would she not tell her what she was going through, no matter how tough.

At that moment, her phone began to ring.

"Hi, Tara!"

"Kika, how are you?"

"I'm okay, just overwhelmed with work and stuff," Kika said mundanely.

"Kika, I think you need to leave your job. I left my job in the law firm to focus on my fashion career. It has been the best decision I ever made in my life - I feel so much more fulfilled," Tara said, exasperated.

"Oh, really?" Kika said sarcastically. Kika was aware of Tara's sudden career change, but Tara had talent, interest in another profession, and Bode's money. All Kika ever wanted to do was write, and writing for the biggest journalism company in Lagos was where she was indeed going to fulfil her dreams.

"You don't have to work for a company that does not see your value or invest in you. Why don't you start a blog or something?" Tara continued.

Kika had thought about that, but starting a blog was not going to pay her bills.

"Well, Tara, we will see. God's will be done."

"Mhmm," Tara said, "Well, just keep doing you."

Kika wondered if Mimi had spoken to Tara about the rumour of Rayo stealing money, but if Tara was not going to mention it, she was not bringing it up either, especially because she did not know whether or not she will be taking the deal with Ms Gozy.

"Look, Kika, my cousin Dabira is staying with me. She came to visit from London. We are going out for drinks on Friday. You are coming, right?"

"Oh, I have always wanted to meet your cousin for the longest time, yes I am up for that."

"I can't get hold of Anita, but I guess she is probably focusing on becoming a new mother?" Tara asked.

"Yeah, probably," Kika was not going to tell Tara anything to do with Anita's situation, "what about Mimi?"

"Erm," Tara paused. "She is busy Friday; she has an event."

"Okay, well, I am super excited. I can't wait," Kika said excitedly, although she could sense something was off.

"Me too! See you Friday! Bye."

After Kika finished the call, she went to have a shower, brushed her teeth, and got ready for bed. She wondered if Tara knew something about Mimi's situation as she felt she was acting weird. Either way, Kika thought she might bring it up on the night out and see what Tara would say.

As she lay in her bed, Kika brought out her journal

from her side table and began to read through what she had written from the mid-week service she attended at church earlier on. She had shared with the group in the past how her boss constantly knocked her confidence and how she has suffered from panic attacks. The leaders always advised her to pray about it and comforted her the best way they could. And now she had been offered everything she had ever prayed for, but Kika knew it just was not right.

[God, should I do it? Are you blessing me with this role, and is betraying Mimi the best way to go about it?]

Kika put her journal down, put off the light, and tried to go to sleep. However, her mind was not at rest, and she could not sleep. All she could think about was how awful it would be for her to participate in Ms Gozy's plan.

"Okay, Lord, I hear you loud and clear. I will not be accepting the offer," she whispered.

Kika was disappointed because she did want the promotion, but losing Mimi, her dignity, and her connection with God was not worth it.

A journal to the reader

Dear Reader,

When you know and understand yourself, you know what makes you tick. You know what hurts you and what brings you joy. You are self-aware. To avoid getting yourself into a negative place, you do your best to avoid situations that will bring you there.

Anita was adamant that she did not want her mum to know about her and Nati's break up. She knew her mum would say things that will aggravate her, and she did not want to be disrespectful or react negatively.

Lo and behold, her mother found out, and although she tried to keep calm, she let her emotions get the best of her, and she reacted out of character.

This leads me to the subject of boundaries. Boundaries keep you self-aware and ensure you are tuned into your emotions. You need to know your limits to avoid pain in the future.

I have to be honest; this is something I am still struggling with. It is very easy for me to get agitated and stressed out. However, I could learn to be more in control of my emotions, and remove myself from the aggravating situation, rather than sit there, allow my blood to boil and flip out.

I have to remember the scripture in Proverbs 15:1 "A soft answer turns away wrath, but a harsh word stirs up anger."

I am a work in progress.

Sometimes it may not be a reaction. You may love watching scary movies, but when you watch them before bed, you are incredibly fearful, and your mind is not at rest. So, you set a boundary to stop watching scary movies before bed.

I remember a few years ago, one of my close friends and I would speak on the phone for hours late at night. She would ring me at 11 pm, and we will finish at like 2:30 am and it would be a school night (actually, a work night). To overcome this, we both

131

agreed to set a boundary for no calls after 10 pm. We did break it a couple of times, but the intent was there and helped us considerably.

What about you? What boundaries do you need to set in your life?

Journal Task 7: Divide a page into two. In the first half, write a list of situations that make you feel good. e.g., "Talking about the future". In the second half, write down a list of situations that make you feel bad. e.g., "bloated, after overeating."

In a different colour, come up with boundaries that will help increase your positive side and decrease your negative side.

For Example:

Positive - Talking about my future. Boundary- Spend an hour a day researching what I want to achieve in the future.

Negative- Overeating. Boundary - Smaller Portions.

Tip: Do not be hard on yourself; we are all a work in progress. Get to know yourself more and be self-aware. One day you will get there.

Lots of Love X

Simi Alexis Romeo

CHAPTER EIGHT

Tara

"Wait here," Tara instructed Dabira. "I want to say bye to Bode."

"Oh, let me come with you," Dabira insisted.

Dabira and Tara were getting ready to leave the house to meet up with Kika for the girls' night-out before Tara suddenly thought to check up on Bode in his study. She still was yet to let Dabira know about their financial issues. One reason being that she did not feel it had anything to do with her, and secondly, because she did not want to give her any insight into the struggle they were facing.

"He is quite swamped with work at the moment, and it will just cause a big distraction if you came in with me."

Dabira gave Tara a quizzical look but agreed to wait at the entrance while Tara went in to see Bode.

Bode had not been himself since the incident regarding Rayo. He refused to eat or sleep, and had vowed not to leave the study until he'd sorted out the financial mess with his lawyers.

"Hey babe, how are you doing?" Tara said, treading carefully. She was adamant about not stepping on Bode's toes.

"I'm still trying to sort this out babe," Bode looked up and saw Tara looking at him from the door to the study. "Wow babe, if there is anything I am grateful for at this moment in time, it's you."

Tara smiled. She was amazed at how Bode could continue to be the most adoring man even when he was going through such a difficult time.

"So, where are you going?" Bode asked.

"Well, Dabira and I are going to meet up with Kika. It was meant to be with all the girls, but Anita is pregnant and Mimi - well, you know."

Bode let out a huge sigh, he did not want to blame Mimi for his issues, as he trusted her and believed she had absolutely nothing to do with it, but he couldn't help the fact that Mimi reminded him of his loss. "You look amazing, darling," he walked up to her and kissed her. "Thank you for always having my back, enjoy your night."

Tara left the room and went downstairs to meet up with Dabira.

"Is everything all okay with Bode?"

"Yes, why would it not be?"

"Tara, remember I know you more than anyone. And when something is bothering you, I know."

Tara knew Dabira was right, but she just could not find the courage to tell her she was virtually broke, especially as Bode was still engaged in trying to sort it all out, anyway.

"We are fine! Honestly, I just want to have a good night," Tara said while dancing and giggling. "I can't wait to get some Hennessy down my system."

Dabira could tell Tara was hiding something, but she

chose not to pry. "When Tara was ready to share, she will share," she thought to herself.

"Oh, speaking of Hennessy, I am taking a little break from alcohol."

Tara looked at Dabira, confused, "why, are you pregnant?"

Dabira laughed, "with what man? Of course, I am not pregnant."

"So, why are you not drinking? I thought we were going to let our hair down together like old times?"

"I know, I was looking forward to it too, but I have a little infection, and I am on antibiotics, which means I am not allowed to take any alcohol. I know it's the worst timing ever."

Tara looked at Dabira with dismay.

"Look, Tara, I am still going to have an incredibly fun night. Don't worry; it will feel like I am drinking too - promise," Dabira assured her.

Tara shrugged her shoulders and let it go. If anything, at least Kika can be her drinking buddy.

"Long Island iced tea, please," Kika ordered from the waitress. "What do you ladies want?"

"Can I please have a gin and tonic and a non-alcoholic Chapman," Tara responded.

This was the first time Kika and Dabira had met. Tara will always speak to her girlfriends about her cousin turned 'sister', Dabira, and how special she was to her. Because Dabira lived in London and was a couple of years younger than her, they never had a chance to meet.

"Oh girls, I have literally had THE worst week," Kika said, taking a sip of her drink.

"What happened?" Tara asked, secretly thinking it probably was not as bad as becoming bankrupt.

"Well, just work, I guess," Kika had made the decision not to sign the contract with Ms Gozy. She knew it was not worth losing her peace, dignity, and friendship over. However, she did not want to tell her friends that she even ever thought about it. Ms Gozy did not take the news well. In fact, she just dropped the phone on Kika.

"I can't repeat it enough; you need to leave and start a blog or something," Tara expressed. "How many times have I told you this?"

Kika nervously giggled. She was tired of her friends saying the same thing. But she knew it was easier said than done.

"So Tara, how are the wedding plans coming along?" Kika asked.

"Yes, it is going well thanks," Tara said nervously.

"Have you picked a date yet?" Kika continued while gesturing to the waitress to order some appetisers.

"No, not yet, we were thinking in about ten months, but nothing is set in stone," Tara responded, "but maybe later, as Dabira brought it to my attention that my family in London need to have time to prepare mentally and financially."

"Yes, I will reiterate that I do think you should give us time, so as many of us as possible can be a part of your big day," Dabira said with a smile.

"Wait - Mimi is your wedding planner, right?" Kika asked quickly while the waiter approached her. "Hi, can we please have some chicken wings, calamari, and some beef sliders."

Tara began to sweat. She knew Kika would have heard about Mimi's husband, Rayo. She was praying she would not bring it up and would have conveniently forgotten about asking the question after she ordered.

Kika turned back to face Tara and Dabira, "What was I saying... yes, so is Mimi your wedding planner?"

"Yes she is, why would I go with any other planner?" She said defensively.

"Well, in that case, I do think you should move your wedding to at least a year from now. There is an investigation going on with Rayo and Mimi. Apparently, Rayo has run away with N5 billion from multiple investors, and no one can find him - not even Mimi."

Dabira's eyes widened.

"I think you should wait for all of this to calm down first before proceeding with the wedding," Kika continued.

"Do you think Mimi had something to do with this?" Dabira asked, panicking, and looking at Tara for a reaction.

"Of course not, We were all pretty sceptical when Mimi started dating Rayo. They got engaged like a month after they met and got married six months after that. He did not grow up like us, which is fine, but it always seemed like he was trying too hard to fit in and will do anything to belong."

"Did you guys ever express your concerns to her about him?" Dabira questioned.

Kika laughed. "Multiple times. In fact, I almost was not invited to the wedding. It was Tara and Anita that told me to shut up and let her live her life."

The girls both turned to look at Tara, who was sitting quietly thinking about everything Kika was saying. Maybe if Tara had just listened to Kika and not deemed her as a 'hater' who was jealous of Mimi and her happiness, then she would not be in the situation she was in.

"Is everything okay, Tara?" Dabira asked as she noticed Tara's eyes welling up.

Tara began to weep. The girls both rushed to either side of her to try and comfort her.

"Don't worry, postponing your wedding to a year from now is not the end of the world," Dabira said.

"Yes - it is probably for the best. At least it gives your family time to come and be a part of it," Kika added.

"It is not just about the wedding, guys," Tara said while wiping her tears.

"So, what is it?" They both asked, confused.

"It's just that, N2 billion of that N5 billion that Rayo stole is Bode's and it's the majority of his funds; I don't think I will be able to have the wedding of my dreams now."

Tara began to cry softly.

Dabira and Kika looked at each other in shock. They were unable to find the words to make the situation better. Kika had heard that the chances of finding Rayo were one in a million. As far as she was concerned, that money was not coming back.

"Tara, look, this is an extremely messy situation, and I know it hurts," Dabira said, breaking the silence.

"Yes, absolutely," Kika interrupted, "even though the chances of getting that money back appear slim, nothing is impossible with God. Plus, Bode is a super smart guy and will probably make that money back in a heartbeat."

"- and you are a super smart girl, you can launch your fashion line and make a name and good money for yourself, too," Dabira added.

"I think what we are both trying to say is, God's hand is constantly on your life, and He works everything out for our good. You are going to come out of this stronger, happier, and grateful that you went through it." Kika finished, hugging Tara tightly.

As the girls were encouraging Tara with words of affirmation from the Bible, she remembered how dismissive she was a few days ago when she spoke to Pastor Lade on the phone. She knew the following morning, she needed to reach out to her, apologise, and prepare to be open. She also knew that at this difficult time, she needed to remain sane for herself and Bode.

Mimi

"I can assure you; I had nothing to do with the article 'Hello Lagos' wrote about you," Kika said frantically, as she walked into Mimi's mother's home, "but Mimi, why did you not tell me?"

Mimi had not told any of her friends about the Rayo scandal as Dami had told her to keep it to herself. Anita was not really picking her phone calls anyways, and Tara was one of the victims and probably hated her guts right this moment.

News of the scandal had gone viral, and all the blogs had picked it up. Mimi's phone had not stopped ringing all day. 'Hello Lagos' had written a story about her and the Rayo situation. Kika had sent her a message that she was coming to visit, and she knew it had to be about the story. Although Mimi felt Kika probably had nothing to do with the article, she was hurt that Kika did not stop it or give her the heads up.

Kika hugged Mimi, "I am so sorry, Mimi. Please trust me when I say I had nothing to do with this. I did not even know they continued the story. I just saw the post on social media."

"Kika, I do trust you." Mimi was not in a position to

doubt her friend's honesty, especially as she was in a similar place where people were questioning hers. "I just want you to know that you are better than 'Hello Lagos'. You should not be a part of such a despicable company that go out of their way to hurt people."

Kika knew Mimi was right, but 'Hello Lagos' was the leading Media House and her dream workplace. She still was not yet ready to give it up.

"So, is what they are saying true?" Kika asked carefully.

"The only incorrect thing was me having anything to do with it," Mimi pleaded her case.

"Oh, my goodness, Mimi, how long has this been going on for?" Kika asked, genuinely concerned.

"About a couple of weeks."

"And you haven't heard from Rayo since he left?"

Mimi shook her head. She did not want to hear from Rayo. She wanted him tracked down and put behind bars for life.

"Kika, he was horrible, and he abused me - he hit me, kicked me, cheated on me, took all my money and called me every name under the sun - and now to make matters worse, he has ruined my life, my business, my reputation, my character, Kika." Mimi looked down and began to cry. She had tried to be strong throughout this whole situation, but her box was full. She could not keep it in any longer.

"Mimi, it is okay to cry, you know, this is not your fault, and we know it. Justice will be served, and God has your back - it will all work out," Kika said while hugging her.

"You know it also affected Tara and Bode," Mimi sniffled, "She says she believes me, but you know how Tara had always desired an extremely affluent life. I literally brought someone into our lives that stole her dream from her. Even if she does not want to blame me, I am sure she will."

"Well, Mimi, I went out with Tara and her cousin Dabira the other night, and I brought up the situation, not knowing she and Bode were victims," Kika said, trying to be honest about her gossiping. "She is not upset with you - trust me."

Mimi looked at Kika; she could not understand why Kika would talk about her issues on a night out with Tara and her cousin, whom none of them knew. "Were you guys gossiping about me?" Mimi finally asked.

"No, it was just from Tara's point of view with the wedding and all?" Kika tried to explain.

"Well, why did you not come to me first?" Mimi asked, getting annoyed with Kika. Although she loved her deeply, she felt Kika loved to gossip. She always had the latest gist and loved to tell the girls about what was going on. Mimi did love hearing the stories, but she was Kika's friend, and she did not expect her to be telling their other friends about her private life.

"I did want to come to you, but I felt because you had not come to me, you may be dealing with a lot and will not have time for a random 'I heard', from me."

"So, you brought it up with Tara and her cousin?"

"Well, I brought it up with Tara because of her wedding plans. I needed to tell her that her wedding was now possibly not going to happen."

Mimi clenched her jaw slightly.

"Look, I am sorry for not coming to you first, but I was not just talking about it as gossip, I was genuinely worried about you and about Tara's wedding," Kika said while placing Mimi's hands in the palm of hers. "Look, the point I am trying to make is Tara genuinely feels bad for you; she is not angry at you. Yes, she hates the situation, but she is happy that you, Daniel, and Desmond escaped such a horrible man. We could have lost you, Mims."

Kika's eyes began to well up, with tears flowing down shortly after. "We love you, Mimi, and we want you to be safe and happy. My heart bleeds for you, dear."

Mimi could see that Kika was coming from a good place. Kika was one of those people who you just could not be upset with for a long period. She loved her, although she feels Kika does need to learn to shut her mouth sometimes.

"I love you too," Mimi said with a smile. "So have you heard from Anita? I have been calling her now for weeks, and she has not been answering the phone."

Kika looked at Mimi and shook her head, "she is probably just focusing on her new life." Kika knew it was not her place to discuss anything to do with Anita's life situation. Anita had begged her not to tell anyone, and anyone included their mutual friends.

"Well, she should count herself lucky. I got a beating because she and Nati did not participate in Rayo's deal. She came to my home, read my 'energy', and called Nati to tell him to reject the deal." Mimi laughed, trying to make light of the situation.

"Wow, well, God is good!" Kika awkwardly laughed. "So, because I know you are going through a tough time, I have made you some 'Cards of Courage' to help you get through the situation."

"Oh wow, I am getting a prototype of these cool 'Cards of Courage'," Mimi joked.

"Oh, absolutely!" Kika gave her a pack of cards, which she quickly opened.

The first card read:

"The Lord is close to the brokenhearted; he rescues those whose spirits are crushed" - *Psalm 34:18.*

The second card read:

"Come to me, all ye who labour and are heavy laden, and I will give you rest" - *Matthew 11:28.*

As Mimi continued to read the cards, she began to feel strangely encouraged.

"Wow Kika, this is just what I need," She said, tearing up again.

Kika smiled.

"I actually wanted to ask you a favour?" Kika said uncomfortably.

"I am listening," Mimi said, looking at Kika.

"I know 'Hello Lagos' is not in your best books right now, but would you consider doing a tell-all interview with us, going through the whole thing, and potentially clearing your name?"

Mimi was shocked at Kika's request.

"Absolutely not, Kika! Rayo will come after me!" She said sternly.

"Okay, I am sorry. It was just an idea!" She was suddenly distracted by Mimi's mother walking into the room. "Good afternoon, ma."

"Oh, Good afternoon, Kika, dear. How are you?" Mrs. Coker asked.

"I am fine, thank, you ma."

"And your parents?" Asked Mrs Coker.

"They are well," Kika smiled, going through the motions of a typical African parent's 'inquisition'.

"That's great to hear." Mrs Coker turned to her daughter, "Demilade, don't forget that Dami is on his way for our meeting, which starts in twenty minutes," she said as she walked back out of the living room.

Mimi had forgotten that Dami was coming over to have a meeting on how to manage the news and control the press, in response to the frenzy on social media.

"Who is Dami?" Kika asked.

"He's my lawyer, very handsome may I just add," Mimi said cheekily poking Kika. Kika was always in and out of relationships with men who never really saw the value in her. It broke Mimi's heart to see her always being mistreated.

"Oh, well, is he single?" Kika asked.

Mimi laughed. She could not believe she had never thought to find that out herself. "I have no idea; he seems single."

Kika hissed, "Most men in Lagos 'seem' single Mimi, do better!" She laughed.

Although Kika was joking, Mimi did think that Kika and Dami would make a good couple. They both took their relationship with God very seriously and worked with the youth in church. They were both hardworking, they were both good looking, and they were both kind. Maybe Kika was right, he probably was not single, or he would have been taken by now.

"Look, let me get out of here before your meeting - but call me anytime," Kika said, hugging her.

Anita

Anita laid in bed, staring at the ceiling, replaying the episode that happened with her mother a few days ago. She felt incredibly guilty for lashing out, as she knew her mum was only coming from a good place and was doing the best she could.

Anita hated dealing with these emotions and was keen to distract herself. She suddenly shook her head in dismay. "I should do something productive today." She said to herself. She got out of bed and walked out of her room to Kika's room and politely knocked on the door.

"Kika, are you there?" She asked.

With no response, she pushed open the door. Kika's room was clean, and her bed was made. She walked around the flat, calling for her, but there was no response.

"Where could she be?" Anita uttered under her breath. Usually, when Kika would leave the house, she would at least say goodbye. She walked over to where she had thrown her phone a few days ago. She picked it up from behind the bedroom door and noticed that the screen was smashed and it wouldn't come on.

"I hope I did not kill it," she sighed as she played with all the buttons. "Of course, battery dead."

She looked around the room for her iPhone charger and suddenly saw the cord hanging out from one of the drawers of the dressing table. She made her way to pick it up when she suddenly noticed a stack of envelopes neatly placed in a pile on the table. She recalled that every single time Kika would bring a tray of food to her, she would always tell her to check under her plate when she finished eating. She was startled at the fact she had forgotten every single time.

She quickly put her phone on charge and proceeded to

open the first envelope, carefully pulling out a pastel pink card with graphical flowers and icons around the perimeter. In the centre was a quote written in foil calligraphy. The back of the card had a logo and a title saying "Loss" and in small letters underneath, it said 'by Kika'.

Anita was flabbergasted as she admired the card. She wondered whether Kika had created this all by herself. She would not be surprised, as she always felt Kika was extremely creative, and it was a shame she was too scared to branch out on her own and do something worthwhile with her gifts and talents. Instead, she was wasting away with the likes of Ms Gozy at 'Hello Lagos'.

Anita began to read the quote on the card.

"Do not be anxious about anything, but in every situation, by prayer and petition, with thanksgiving, present your requests to God. And the peace of God, which transcends all understanding will guard your hearts and your minds in Christ Jesus." Philippians 4: 6-7.

As Anita read the verse, she instantly felt encouraged as it related to what she was going through.

She realised it was, in fact, a scripture from the Bible and not just any ordinary quote. She could not understand why she felt this way as she did not see herself as religious in any way whatsoever. She was secretly curious to see the other cards.

She opened the next envelope and pulled out the card. This time it was a peach coloured one.

> *"Trust in the Lord with all your heart and lean not on your own understanding; in all your ways submit to him and he will direct your paths" Proverbs 3: 5-6.*

"But who exactly am I trusting?" Anita thought to herself, "Direct my paths? Hmm," she picked up the next card from the envelope below.

> *"…weeping may endure for a night, but joy comes in the morning" Psalm 30:5.*

Anita wondered why Kika would send her scriptures from the Bible when she knew she was not interested in Christianity at all. The other thing she couldn't fathom was why the cards encouraged her so. Why did she feel a sense of peace? For some reason, these scriptures were able to relate to her current situation, and she felt an assurance that everything was going to be alright.

She looked over at her charging phone, which had now come on. Unbothered by the cracks in the screen and the 40 missed calls she had from Nati, she scrolled down her contact list to Kika's number and began to dial.

"Hey, Anita! How are you?" Kika asked.

"Hey Kika, where are you?" she said in a soft voice.

"I am just leaving Mimi's house. I went to church and thought to stop by at hers on the way back - it is Sunday, remember," Kika laughed. "I did go into your room earlier on to invite you, but you were fast asleep, and I did not want to wake you," Kika said, smiling.

Anita was happy that Kika had indeed tried to see her

before she left. However, she was also confused - why did Kika keep on inviting her to church all the time?

"Kika?" She said, "you know I am not a Christian, why would you think I would go?"

"Because…," she chose her words wisely and said calmly, "what you are going through is tough, and no one can comfort you the way you need to be comforted other than Jesus."

"But, you are comforting me just fine?" Anita said, thinking smartly.

"I am doing the best I can, but there are going to be times I will not be available, and you will really need to speak to someone. God is never too busy for you, so it is important to nurture that relationship with him."

Anita thought about what Kika had said and was lost for words. She quickly proceeded to change the topic.

"So anyway, I need you to please explain what those cards you gave me are supposed to mean?"

Kika smiled, realising that Anita had finally opened the envelopes she had been leaving on her food trays. "Oh, so you finally had time to read the cards," Kika said sarcastically.

"Yes, I have, sorry. I just noticed them," Anita said, a bit embarrassed.

"Well, what do you think?"

"So, is this a business you are starting?" Anita asked, trying not to focus too much on the scriptures.

"Yes! So, I had this idea a while ago. As you know, I absolutely adore 'words' and also love to encourage women. I realised that the entries in my journal from years back tend to support me through difficult times when I go back to read them, especially when I need an instant reminder. So, I thought, why not develop the idea and create 'Cards of Courage'. I thought to try the

'Cards of Courage' idea out on you, given your current situation. So, what do you think?" Kika asked once again.

"What do you mean, what do I think, aren't these for Christians? I am not a Christian, Kika!" Anita exclaimed, reminding Kika again.

"Well, it is for everyone to be honest," assured Kika. "You are obviously going through a tough time, as I said. I know from past experiences that when you are going through these times, no one can really comfort you as much as God. You cannot rely on human beings because they are not perfect for one, and can be busy at times as they all have one thing or another going on in their lives," Kika said, thinking about how both Mimi and Tara's lives had changed significantly. "I felt by creating these cards for you with words of encouragement - it would lift your spirit. It will give you a sense of hope and assure you that you do have worth, you are super-valued, and God has big plans for your life."

Anita was speechless. She was completely confused.

"What?!" Laughed Kika, "The scriptures helped, didn't they?"

Anita shrugged her shoulders. Kika was right. It did really touch her, even if she did not want to admit it to her friend.

"Okay, smartypants, what's next?"

"How do you mean?" Asked Kika.

"Well, you obviously gave me these scriptures for a reason, so what would you like me to do next?" Anita asked.

"Look, it's not about me wanting you to do anything in particular. I just want you to feel better. You can happily have these scriptures and keep going through them - if that is enough for you, then great. If you want to understand more about the root of these scriptures, then maybe you can accompany me to church one day?"

The thought of attending church scared Anita, but she did want to understand more about the scriptures. "I think church is a bit much for me - I have not attended a church service in years, and I do not feel I would be comfortable, so I guess I would just deal with scriptures and try to understand them myself."

"If it makes it easier, maybe you can come to our mid-week service on Wednesday. It is a smaller group - about 12 of us, and you can ask as many questions as you feel led to ask. What do you say?"

That idea was a lot more appealing to Anita. A small group meant a lot more discussion, which she felt she needed. "Sure, let's do that!"

Anita ended the call abruptly before she could change her mind. She looked at the scriptures again and was perplexed that she could still feel the sense of comfort.

"Strange," she uttered to herself. She, however, was looking forward to Wednesday's mid-week service. "Maybe God is real?" She thought. But she would not say it out loud.

Kika

As Kika got off the phone with Anita, she was in great spirits. Anita's call to say she finally read the cards and was interested in coming to church was very exciting. She had also just shown Mimi the 'Cards of Courage', and Mimi had teared up. For Kika, this was terrific progress as it meant the cards worked. It helped people going through difficult times, which was what she wanted.

"Wow God, if this is not you, I do not know who it is?" Kika gushed.

As Kika was driving out of Mimi's estate in Victoria Garden City (VGC), a beautiful suburb of Lagos, she had a minor collision with a black Range Rover vehicle.

"Oh my goodness, are you for real!" She screamed. Kika was furious. She stepped out of her car and approached the driver's door. The person remained in the car, and Kika tapped on the tinted window.

"These crazy Nigerian drivers," she said to herself. It was, however, loud enough for the driver to hear. He began to wind down the window slowly, and to her surprise, he was nothing like she was expecting. The man was probably in his 30s, pushing 40. He had plenty of facial hair, gorgeous skin, and a good haircut. In fact, when he wound down his windows, she could smell his nice cologne wafting out of the car.

Kika had been expecting it to be one of these young twenty-something-year-old types, carelessly driving cars they could not afford.

"Excuse me, do you not have the decency to come out after hitting my car?" Kika blurted out in frustration.

"Hit your car? You hit my car! I am not coming out because I am late for an appointment," the man responded.

Kika could not believe how arrogant this man was being. First, he hit her car, then he didn't have the decency to apologise, but instead, was actually blaming her.

"I am so sorry that you hit my car and are unable to take responsibility because you feel you are the only one that has stuff to do today. So sorry!" Kika said in a sardonic way.

The man sighed. He realised that Kika was not the type of person just to let it go. The sooner he came out of the car, the sooner he would be able to sort the situation and be on his way.

As he opened the door and came out of the car, Kika could not help but notice how gorgeous this man was. He was tall, had a good body, and was very attractive. She immediately sneaked a look at his ring finger. It was bare; she smirked a little before remembering that just because you are not wearing a ring does not mean you are not taken in Lagos, Nigeria.

Realising that she was awkwardly smiling at the man, she shook her head, "Now that's better!"

"So did I scratch your car?" The guy did not feel the accident was his fault. He had indicated that he was turning into the estate, whereas Kika just came out without looking.

"Well, let's have a look, shall we?" Kika knew her car was not scratched, but it was about common decency and the principle of it. You hit someone, you come out and apologise.

"Your car looks fine to me," The man said. "So are we good?"

Kika rolled her eyes, "Are you not going to apologise?"

"For what? You came out of the junction without looking or indicating and ended up hitting my car?"

Kika gasped, "I had the right of way, sir - I did not need to indicate."

The man looked at his watch, "Look, I have to go. I really do not have time for this."

"Then apologise!" Kika roared as she stood on her toes to level her eyes with his. She was not backing down from this one. Lucky for her, she had all day.

The man sighed, "I am sorry for hitting your car." Kika giggled a little as he apologised. It was clearly so painful for him to apologise, and she loved every second of it.

"I can see you are enjoying yourself. So, are we good?" The man said, putting his hand out for a handshake.

Kika smiled, "I accept your apology." She reciprocated the handshake and watched the man jump into his car and speed off.

As Kika got back into her car, she was annoyed that she did not manage to get his name. He was the most beautiful man she had seen in a long time and the fact that her charm got her what she wanted - in this case, an apology - meant that they would make a perfect couple, she felt.

"A girl can only dream," she mused to herself.

Kika began to make her way back to her apartment in Lekki, but all she could think about was his eyes, his beauty, the way he spoke.

"Oh my goodness, what is wrong with me?" Kika hated it when she obsessed over a guy, especially someone she barely knew. For all she knows, he could be married with deep issues, maybe not even share her faith, "Oh God, please help me to be focused. If it is meant to be, it would be," she prayed.

As Kika walked into her apartment, she was pleasantly surprised to see Anita in the living room, eating jollof rice and chicken while watching a movie.

"Hey girl, I missed you all day," Anita said as she worked her way through her chicken bone.

Kika went towards Anita and hugged her.

"How was church?" Anita asked.

"Church was good. I saw Mimi afterward, she said she has been trying to get hold of you."

"You did not tell her anything about Nati and the baby, did you?" Anita asked nervously.

"No, literally nobody knows."

"Good!" Anita said, continuing to eat her chicken.

Kika could not understand why Anita did not want to tell her best friends about her current situation. The whole gang was going through one thing or another, and nobody wanted to be open. Kika was frustrated because she felt that friends were meant to have each other's back in the good times and be there in your hardest times.

"I am so hungry, I am going to get a plate of jollof rice myself," Kika said.

"It is so good, I might have another plate." Anita joked.

Kika laughed while walking into the kitchen to get herself a plate. Her phone then started to ring.

"Really, on a Sunday, Ms Gozy is calling me?" she screamed.

"Don't pick it up Kika, this woman needs to respect your time and pay you for it!" Anita yelled from the living room.

Ever since she chose not to go with Ms Gozy's deal, Kika had felt the tension between them. 'Hello Lagos' had revealed the story of Mimi's situation but included lies about her involvement. But Kika felt at peace for not being associated with it. The promotion would not have been worth it.

"Don't pick it up o!" Anita yelled, again.

Kika saw Anita's point but decided to pick up the call. She was already on thin ice, and she did not want to make it any worse.

"Good afternoon, Ms Gozy," Kika said boldly.

"Kika, I am calling you to give you one more chance, and I hope you will not disappoint me today," Ms Gozy said on the phone.

Kika's heart began to beat. "What was Ms Gozy going to ask her to do this time?" She thought to herself.

"I will try not to," Kika said awkwardly.

"Kika, do not! I have heard that Tara Williams and Bode Cole were affected by Rayo Abraham's fraud. I hear N2 billion. Is this true?"

Kika leaned on the kitchen counter. Why did Ms Gozy feel that it was okay to put her in these situations? Why would she expect her to throw her friends under the bus?

"I have not heard anything," Kika lied.

"Well, find out quickly. You are our inside scoop!" She said excitedly.

Kika realised she had to be real with Ms Gozy. Ms Gozy needed to understand that it is not in her nature to betray her friends - even if her dream job is in jeopardy.

"Ms Gozy, I need to be honest with you," Kika said apprehensively.

"What is wrong?" Ms Gozy asked.

"Ms Gozy, I really am serious about my job at 'Hello Lagos'. I also really admire you for creating such a top firm. But I have to be honest; I will never release any information about my close friends and family, no matter the incentive - I do not even want to be part of the firm's gossip section. I am a Christian and wish only to report the truth or provide advice - you know, positive things."

Ms Gozy was silent on the other end of the call.

"Hello, Ms Gozy, are you there?" She said anxiously.

"Kika! I am just fed up with you!" She dropped the phone abruptly.

Kika covered her plate of rice and put it in the fridge. All of a sudden, her appetite was gone. There was a high probability she had just lost her job.

A journal to the reader

Dear Reader,

Stress balls were created to allow individuals to deal with stress. A person will take the ball, squeeze it with everything they've got, and release, but it will bounce back into shape. This is a practical example of what resilience is.

All the ladies are going through a tough period at the moment. The pressures of life are squeezing them with everything it's got. Now it's their choice to either dwell in that state or release the worries to God so they can bounce back.

Growing up, I did not get the best grades. I failed a lot of tests and exams, or I would just about pass, barely. Sometimes it was my fault due to the fact that I did not study, but at other times, I would make an effort, and the results would not show that.

I remember in 2013, I had just finished my second year in university. I had worked so hard on my end of year exams.

When the results came out in the summer, I had failed one of my exams - I was heartbroken. I remember calling my dad to tell him that university wasn't for me, and I wanted to drop out. But with God's help 'and some encouragement from my dad' (Lol - he put this in here), I was able to bounce out of that emotional state and start revising for my re-sit test. I ended up passing, and I progressed into my 3rd year.

Although I had struggled during my whole academic journey, I never for once felt I could not do it. I always felt the next test and exam would be better. There was a shift in my story when I graduated after my third year, as I ended up finishing with a First-Class. Everyone around me was in shock. I wasn't; I was happy I had proven to others what I had always believed in myself. I always felt that I could do all things through Christ who strengthens me. (Philippians 4:13)

You cannot control the pressures in life that come your way, *but you can control how you let it affect you. Holding negative thoughts and constant worrying is not healthy for your mind, soul, or body.*

If you are worried about something and you can do something about it, then do it.

If you are worried about something and you cannot do anything about it, then there is no point in worrying.

The bible states in Luke 12:25, "Who of you by worrying can add a single hour to your life? Since you cannot do this very little thing, why do you worry about the rest?"

It also states how God is in control of everything, and all we need to do is continue to seek him.

Luke 12:29- 31 says: "Do not set your heart on what you will eat or drink; do not worry about it. For the pagan world runs after all such things, and your Father knows that you need them. But seek his kingdom, and these things will be given to you as well."

Journal Task 8: In journal 5, you wrote down a list of things you may be struggling with at the moment. Positive thoughts and knowing God is in control can help you bounce back from this. Write down positive scenarios that can come out from the setback you are facing. Ask God for the grace to help bring about these positive outcomes.

Tip: "Do not be anxious about anything, but in every situation, by prayer and petition, with thanksgiving, present your requests to God." - Philippians 4:6.

Lots of Love X

Simi Alexis Romeo

CHAPTER NINE

Tara

"Good morning Pastor Lade, would I be able to come to your office today for a session?" Tara said on the phone.

After the events of the night-out the other week with Kika and Dabira, Tara knew she owed Pastor Lade an apology. She realised that she had only been trying to help her become a better woman and prepare her for the next stage of her life. Luckily for Tara, Pastor Lade had not given up on her. She had always been compassionate and saw the good in her.

"Of course, Tara, Should I get my husband to come too for Bode?"

"No, I would actually like a private session for just the two of us."

Although Pastor Lade was not expecting Tara to choose to speak to her only, she was happy that she now seemed to see the benefit of counselling and had also realised that she had only been coming from a place of love.

"Absolutely, I have a slot this afternoon at 3 pm if you can make it?"

"That's perfect!"

Tara was anxious about going through counselling. She felt she had years of negative emotions buried inside of her. She was now about to let Pastor Lade into her messy mind to see, but it was the only way she could see herself getting through this.

She walked out of her bedroom to Bode's office to see whether he wanted something to eat and to tell him she was meeting Pastor Lade later that day. To her surprise, Bode was not there. He had barely left the study ever since Rayo had run off with the money. He was determined to come up with a solution before dealing with the outside world, and although Tara did not feel there was much that he could do, she admired and respected his determination.

"Morning, cuz! How are you?" Dabira said, catching Tara by surprise.

"Hey Dabira, have you seen Bode this morning? He is not in his office," Tara asked nervously.

"Yes, I saw him rushing out of the house this morning. He seemed very dazed and distracted," Dabira said, pondering. "Maybe he has found a solution to all this mess."

Dabira was doing her best to avoid bringing up the fact that Tara and Bode had lost a lot of money. She had known Tara since she was a child, and Tara always dreamt of the rich and fabulous lifestyle. She knew that losing all this money had to be her worst nightmare.

"Well, he said he wouldn't leave the office until he had a solution, so maybe he does?" Tara said, smiling.

Without waiting to hear Dabira's response, Tara excitedly ran to her bedroom to find her phone to give Bode a call. As she got into the room, her phone started to ring from within the rolls of her unmade duvet. She wrestled with the sheets before finally coming up with the phone, only to see that she had just missed a call from Anita. Tara rolled her eyes. Why was Anita calling her? Did Anita call to gloat about the fact that she and her husband are still the wealthiest family within their friendship group? Tara was not ready to descend into a bad mood, especially when there was a high chance her financial mess was about to be sorted.

She quickly sent Anita a text message. [Hey girl, I saw your call. Just busy atm. I will call you shortly.] Tara closed their chat and proceeded to give Bode a call.

"Hey, dear."

"Hey babe, I went into your office, and you weren't there. Where are you?" Tara asked, concerned.

"Sorry, I should have told you. I went to the gym," Bode was always quick to take responsibility and smooth things over when it came to Tara, especially when he knew he was wrong. "This whole thing is stressing me out, as you can imagine. Needed to blow off some steam. I will be home soon."

A bit of Tara was sad that things had not turned around in the financial sector, but she was happy her husband was dealing with the stress in the right way.

"That's fine, baby. Just to let you know I have a private counselling session with Pastor Lade this afternoon. I think it would be good to kind of work on some of my issues. I want to be whole and happy, so I can be the perfect wife to you".

"Aww, darling, that is music to my ears." Bode said with a smile. "Counselling is so important for couples. I know this change is hard on both of us. I am very proud of you."

Tara finished the call, grinning from ear to ear. She was a child at heart, and her love language was words of affirmations. She loved it when Bode approved of her and was proud. She went into the bathroom to get ready for her afternoon session with Pastor Lade.

"Thanks for coming, Tara, please take a seat," Pastor Lade said with a smile.

Tara sat down on the comfortable sofa she usually shares with her fiancé. She crossed her legs and placed her hands on her lap before slowly beginning to play with her finger and fingernails - something she does whenever she feels nervous.

"So, what made you change your mind about counselling, and what has brought you here?" Pastor Lade asked.

"Well, I don't know if you have heard, but Bode has pretty much lost his entire fortune to a scammer who happens to be one of my best friends husband."

"Oh yes, I heard about Motunrayo Abraham - your wedding planner's husband?" Pastor Lade said, trying not to show that she was aware of the gossip going around town.

Tara nodded, "well, it was pretty much all of Bode's money, he said I needed to cut back on everything. My cousin Dabira said that it is important now for me to step up to the plate financially. I know if I do that, Bode will be proud of me."

Pastor Lade looked at Tara, "Tara, why do you feel the need to seek approval from others?"

Tara looked at Pastor Lade; she was perplexed. She could not understand how anything she had just said could be construed to mean seeking approval from anybody.

Pastor Lade could see the confusion on Tara's face

"You should know that Bode will be incredibly proud of you no matter what. You do not have to put this pressure on yourself."

"Yes, of course, he would. He is my husband-to-be at the end of the day," Tara agreed. "But I think what I mean is I have to prove that at this difficult time, I am there for him."

"Tara, he knows that you are there for him. He asked you to marry him, didn't he?"

Tara looked down at her hands and continued to play with each finger at a time. She just felt Pastor Lade was not getting her. She felt perhaps it was because she was using the wrong choice of words.

Pastor Lade could see she was getting uncomfortable, so she decided to change the subject. "Tara, how do you feel about cutting back?"

Tara sighed, "Erm well, I just feel like, of course, it was going to happen to me. If anyone is going to get scammed and be reduced to absolutely nothing - it's me!"

"But why would you say that?" Pastor Lade asked, a bit surprised.

"Well, it is obvious, that has always been my story. It's like I can never come out on top. There are always others who are better than me, and Pastor Lade, I am sick and tired of it!" Tara said, taken aback that she actually expressed these thoughts she always kept buried deep inside of her.

"So when you say it is your story, can you explain and maybe give some examples?" Pastor Lade treaded softly to avoid any backlash from Tara.

"Well, it all started from childhood. I came into the world unwanted and hated," Tara's voice began to choke up. "My own mother could not stand me, which I understand - I remind her of her deepest hurt. I ruined her happy life!"

Pastor Lade was taken aback by Tara's words. She had no idea what she was referring to.

Tara picked up on this and went on to say, "I am a product of rape, Pastor. My mother wanted nothing to do with me. She rejected me three times. At first, she wanted to abort me, my grandma pleaded with her; then when I was born she wanted to send me to an orphanage, but my grandma kept me, and when my grandma died she wanted to give me up again, but her sister who is my aunty decided to keep me."

Pastor Lade did not know how to respond as she was stunned by this unexpected revelation. She had suspected Tara was troubled, and something was bringing her down, but she did not expect something of this magnitude.

"Wow, I am so sorry to hear this, Tara, how is everything with your mum now?" Pastor Lade asked.

"We do not talk, she cannot even stand to look at me, and to be honest, I am fine with it," Tara said strongly.

Pastor Lade knew Tara did not feel like this. "When was the last time you saw her?"

"I saw her a few months ago at my grandma's memorial."

"Well, did you talk?"

"We said hi. Look, Pastor Lade, this woman hates me. As I said, I remind her of the most hurtful thing she ever experienced, so I understand."

Pastor Lade nodded, "Look, Tara, what your mother went through was very painful, and it was probably the hardest thing she had ever experienced. However, a blessing came out of it - that blessing is you. Think about Jesus Christ, who died for our sins. We did wrong, he suffered through it, but a blessing came out of it. Now we are forgiven and free."

Tara continued to look down and play with her fingers. She had never seen it this way before. She always knew the story of Jesus Christ dying for her sins, but she had not realised that her story was in any way similar.

"I know your mother blaming you for all of this is not fair, but I think you need to forgive her for your sake. You may think you are over it, but it is impacting your life, and you cannot continue to be a victim of somebody else's errors. Do not see yourself as a mistake. You are a delight - I think so, your friends think so, and Bode knows so," Pastor Lade comforted.

Tara looked up at Pastor Lade and smiled at her. "So, how do I forgive her?" She asked.

"Well, maybe reach out to her. She needs to forgive this person that hurt her all these years ago. Maybe even bring her here, and we can all talk," Pastor Lade said, trying to convince her.

"Okay, maybe I will," Tara was uplifted by the session she had just had, "Thank you so much, Pastor Lade." She stood up, and they hugged. She felt like some weight had been lifted off her shoulders. Although she was a bit anxious about reaching out to her mother, she felt that Pastor Lade was going to get her through it all, somehow.

"It's okay Tara, please feel free to call me anytime," she said with a smile.

Mimi

"I have been receiving death threats!" Mimi said to Dami, crying. "I had about seven new customer meetings this month, and they have all been cancelled because of all the hate I am getting. I am also way too scared to leave the house for the job engagements I already have. There doesn't appear to be any way I can make a living for myself and the boys."

Dami sighed. He could understand Mimi's pain. This was the hardest case he had ever handled in his ten years of practice as a lawyer. The world was angry with Mimi when her only sin was that she fell in love with the wrong person.

"Look, from the beginning, I told you this was not going to be easy, and Mimi, you are like a sister to me - I don't want to see you hurt." He sighed. "I have been in touch with the police and private investigators, and we jointly came up with one potential solution, but I am not sure how you will feel about it?"

Mimi looked up at Dami nervously, "what is the solution?"

"We were thinking to maybe interview with one of the leading media houses to explain your side of the story."

Mimi's eyes widened, "I can't do that, Dami! He will come after me!" Mimi shrieked, thinking of Rayo's rage.

"Exactly! We need him to come back so we can try to track him down. I understand it is terrifying, but we will do everything to protect you."

Mimi was at a loss for words. Rayo could decide to hurt anyone she was remotely close to. And he may not strike straight away; it could be months and maybe even years. Will they all be protecting her then too?

"Look, I understand that this is not ideal, but you will be able to clear your name, get your business back, and help find Rayo, hopefully getting all the money back," Dami maintained.

Mimi thought about what Dami was saying. The good definitely does appear to outweigh the bad, but she was scared. The abuse from Rayo - punching her, slapping her

- happened when she barely did anything. But to boldly stand up and declare to the world everything he had done, she would probably die.

"Demilade, I agree with Dami," Mrs Coker said, walking into the room, not trying to hide the fact that she had been eavesdropping on their whole conversation, "Be bold, be strong for the Lord your God is with you."

Mimi gulped.

"Do it for your boys, Mimi," encouraged Dami.

Mimi looked at Dami and her mother and began to declare a scripture that she had read on Kika's 'Cards of Courage' under her breath.

"Say to those with fearful hearts, be strong, and do not fear, for your God is coming to destroy your enemies. He is coming to save you" Isaiah 35: 4.

Mimi knew coming out in an interview was pretty much asking for a brutal retribution from Rayo, but she did not want to be a slave to fear. She wanted to be strong for herself and her boys.

"Okay, I will do it!"

"Okay, are you ready," Roma, the popular interviewer from the media outlet 'The Roma Show', asked Mimi.

"I have never been more ready," she said, smiling.

"Action…!"

Her mother sat close by to give her emotional support during the filming of the show.

Mimi spoke about everything from the beginning. She

talked about how she met Rayo and how everyone was against their relationship, but because the love she felt was so strong for him, she refused to listen to what anyone had to say.

She spoke about getting married and how Rayo's true personality slowly began to show - she shared everything in great detail. How he would slap her senseless, how he would push her over and use her as a punching bag, and how he took all her money and assumed complete control of all her finances.

She went on to describe how he controlled every aspect of her life - he decided what job she took, and where she could and could not go. She explained that what hurt her the most was that she was unable to stop him from taking advantage of her friends and family. Mimi gave a heartfelt apology to all those who were defrauded by Rayo and expressed how she herself is in a similar position financially, how she had to move back in with family members, and didn't have the money to sustain herself and her sons. She assured the intended viewers that she definitely was not living off of what others have lost.

Mimi spoke from the heart and left out no details. She even mentioned how speaking out was, in effect, putting her life at risk.

When she had finished, she found she was in high spirits. She found that being bold and speaking out had turned out to be therapeutic.

"You did well, Mimi. Congratulations on becoming a free bird," Dami said, smiling and hugging her.

"I am proud of you Demilade," Mrs Coker said, kissing her daughter on the cheek.

"Thank you so much. I am extremely proud of myself, as well. I cannot believe I did this. I just hope I will not start to suffer again from anxiety when the interview airs." Mimi said, rubbing her chest.

"Let me get you some hot chamomile tea with a teaspoon of honey. That should hopefully calm your nerves." Mrs Coker said, walking into the kitchen.

As she left, Mimi felt it was the perfect opportunity to ask Dami a question that had been playing on her mind. "Dami are you single?"

Dami looked over at Mimi and laughed, "who's asking?"

"I was thinking of introducing you to one of my best friends," Mimi said quickly to ensure that he did not think she was interested.

"And that friend happens to be…?"

Mimi gave Dami a distressed look, why could he not just answer the question?

"Yes, I am single, been single for a few years, and I have never been married. Oh, and no kids too, may I just add," he said, making jest of the question.

"Well, in that case, you should definitely meet my friend Kika. I think you two will be perfect for each other." Mimi said, feeling proud that she could play matchmaker.

"Hmm," Dami thought, "Why don't you set up a dinner or something casual to avoid any awkwardness," Dami suggested. He was open to meeting new people.

"It could be my celebration dinner when the interview comes out," Mimi laughed.

"That's a fantastic idea," Dami said.

Anita

"Can we all please say a word of prayer before we begin this session."

Anita closed her eyes tightly and put her hands

together like she used to do when she attended Sunday School as a child. She listened to Ola attentively as she opened the session with a prayer. Ola was the leader of Kika's mid-week service - also known as fellowship. She seemed quite jovial and also caring - which is what she felt she needed.

When Ola had finished praying, she continued by introducing Anita.

"Ladies, we have a new guest today. She is a good friend of our dear friend, Kika. Can we all welcome, Anita!" The room of twelve women all turned to face Anita. They began to give her a round of applause while smiling and waving.

"Kind of creepy," Anita whispered to Kika, who was clapping next to her, smiling.

"They are just being friendly Ani, be open!" Kika whispered back.

Anita forged a smile at the other ladies.

"Anita, introduce yourself, what brings you to our fellowship, and what would you like to gain from this experience?" Asked Ola.

Anita became exceptionally nervous. She had taken the courage to accompany Kika to her mid-week service as she was determined to receive answers to specific questions. However, she did not feel ready to open up to a room of twelve women she did not know.

"Hi everyone," she nervously stated, "my name is Anita Fawun-Edoh," she began to stutter. Usually, when she introduced herself, she would always follow up with how she was married to the most amazing husband, but now she was unsure of her marital status. She also did not have any children or a job, and it suddenly hit her - there was nothing she felt was going on in her life.

Kika gently rubbed Anita's back as she could sense that

she was getting uncomfortable. This kind gesture pushed Anita to begin to cry. At that moment, the girls all surrounded her and gave her hugs to try to comfort her.

"No matter what you are going through, Anita, Jesus loves you, and he has not brought you here by accident. I know we just met, but we are your sisters, and we are here for you," Ola said, hugging her again. All the girls nodded and tried to encourage Anita as best they could.

She smiled, "Thank you all. I really appreciate it."

Ola continued with the session - the topic was God's perfect love.

Anita found this topic inspirational. What resonated with her most was how God's love supposedly never fails and how there is no fear in love. So, therefore, 'perfect love drives out fear.'

Growing up, Anita had believed that her purpose and goal in life was to be a wife and a mother. Although she received exceptional grades in school, a first-class honours degree at university, and enjoyed singing and dancing as hobbies, her mother would tell her that these skills were not for pursuing dreams, but for when she accompanies her husband to dinner parties and events. "Everyone needs to know that your husband married a smart wife." Her mother would always say.

Anita always felt the need to compare herself to her friends who were working or had businesses or had children. She suspected that the true reason she did not achieve much was that she was so fearful. The big question on her mind was whether she ever really loved herself? She had always allowed the security of her father or her husband to make her feel secure.

Now that all these had failed and she hadn't become a mother, she felt as though she was worthless. If she truly loved herself, she would not have allowed fear to stop her from having goals and dreams and striving to achieve them.

At the end of the session, Ola walked up to Kika and Anita to find out how they found it.

"It was captivating, Ola, thanks so much," Kika said ecstatically.

"That's great, Kika. What about you, Anita? I apologise if you felt I put you on the spot at the start of the session," Ola said, feeling remorseful.

"Oh no, not at all - it was great. I will definitely be coming back," Anita said with a smile. She felt the session gave her a bit of clarity about her life and where she was going, and she was keen to find out more.

Later that evening, Anita was replaying the session from the mid-week service in her head. She was baffled by how a lot of things started to make sense. She reached for her old pregnancy journal on her bedside table to go through the notes she made from the session. She always felt she loved herself and had confidence, but the fact that she hid behind Nati's shadow all these years proved that she had underlying fears. "Do I love myself?" She asked.

There was a knock on the door.

"Come in!" Anita shouted. She knew it was Kika.

"Hey love, What are you reading?" Kika asked.

"Hey, Kika, it was so strange how many gems Ola dropped today." She walked over to where Kika was standing and put her hands on her shoulders. "Kika, you know me more than anyone. Do you think I have lost myself? Be honest."

Kika was not expecting this question at all. The honest truth was she did feel that Anita changed when she married Nati. Anita had so much going for her. But she had gotten married early, and her life became all about him and his career and supporting his dreams. However, Kika felt she could not bring this up because she knew Anita would throw the 'single' card and tell her she does not understand because she is not married and had never been a wife.

"I do not think you have lost yourself completely, I just feel you do not pursue the things you used to enjoy when we were younger," Kika said cautiously.

There was a long pause. "You know you are right! I do not know if being a wife will cut it as I do not know if that part of my life still exists. You need to help me get back to my old self, please!"

Kika was pleased to hear this as she always wanted the best for her friend. "Okay. Well, let us start with church."

"Church? I was never into church - that is not going back to my old self."

"Exactly. We do not want you to go back - we want you to move forward," Kika smiled. "At church, I teach ages two to four in Sunday school - there is an opening for an assistant. I think it is perfect because we mainly sing and dance, plus you will be with me the whole time. What do you say?"

Anita looked anxiously at Kika, "But I do not know how to take care of kids - I have no kids of my own."

"Hellooo? Neither do I," Kika responded. "But I know you love children, and you love to sing. Why don't you try it out this Sunday, and if you do not like it, we can look into something else." Kika hoped that Anita would be convinced. "Come on, Ani…".

"Okay, let's do it. This Sunday at church."

Sunday had arrived, and Kika and Anita were walking into the children's classroom. Just as they were about to enter, Anita became agitated.

"Are you okay?" Asked Kika.

"Yes, I am fine. I just hope the children like me."

"Trust me, they will love you. Just follow my lead; you will do great!" Assured Kika.

"Thank you, Kiks." Anita smiled.

They walked into the classroom and began to prepare for the lesson. Slowly, parents began to drop off their kids.

"Hello, would you like to do some colouring?" Kika would say to the children to distract them from the fact their parents were leaving the classroom. The children smiled and followed Kika to the arts and crafts table. Anita admired how Kika worked well with children. She stood back and watched how the children were given a picture of Noah's ark to colour in.

"Anita, please come over and help the children with their colouring," Kika said to her.

"What, me?" Anita asked, confused, pointing at herself.

"Yes, you!" Kika laughed, "don't be scared; they are not going to bite," she joked.

Anita walked up to the craft table and bent down.

"Hello, children, I am aunty Anita," she said slowly.

One of the children looked up at Anita and beamed. He was a little boy who was a lot smaller than the other children. He picked up his sheet and waved it in Anita's face and smiled.

Anita immediately felt a deep connection with the child.

"Wow! Your colouring looks amazing! What is your name?" She asked.

The little boy looked back at his worksheet very proudly.

"So this is Caleb," Kika responded. "He was born prematurely, and he is an orphan. One of the leaders in the church owns an orphanage of about 30 children - all different ages. They bring the children here every Sunday," Kika said to Anita, whispering to ensure the kids did not hear her.

Anita looked into the boy's big brown eyes. He was so cute; how can someone just give him up?

"Alright, children, we are now going to sing some songs, let's get into a big circle," Kika called out to the children.

Anita assisted Kika by ensuring all the children cooperated and formed a circle.

Kika began singing 'He's got the whole world in His hands' while doing the actions to rhyme with the words. And the children all followed, singing and copying Kika's actions - they opened their arms as wide as they could to symbolise having the whole world. Anita found she was having the most fantastic time - dancing and laughing with the children.

"Okay, children, aunty Anita is going to give us a new song," Kika said, aware she was putting Anita on the spot.

Anita looked apprehensively at Kika. The last time she remembered singing any gospel music, she was only eleven. "Erm, 'This little light of mine'?" Anita looked at Kika for assurance.

"Okay, sing it then," Kika urged.

Anita began to sing 'This little light of mine'. She also quickly came up with easy steps for the children to follow, and soon they were all singing and dancing, copying Anita's steps. The kids were laughing and having fun, which melted Anita's heart.

At the end of the service, the parents came in one by one to collect their children. Caleb was sitting by himself, doing some drawing as he waited for his housemother. Anita walked over and sat next to him.

"Hi, Caleb, what are you drawing?"

Caleb looked over at Anita and smiled, "The whole world."

"Oh, like the song we sang earlier - it looks beautiful - well done."

Caleb continued to draw quietly.

"So how old are you?" Anita asked.

Caleb smiled and placed four tiny fingers in Anita's face.

"Oh, wow, you're a big boy, aren't you?" Anita laughed.

Kika could see Anita and Caleb were forming a beautiful bond, which unfortunately had to be broken once Caleb's house mother arrived.

"Caleb, Madame Pat is here!" Kika called.

Caleb jumped up, smiled at Anita, and ran to Madame Pat. Madame Pat was a lady in her 60s, and a leader in church, who had been running the orphanage for over twenty years.

"Caleb was such a delight," Kika told Madame Pat.

"Thank you so much. He enjoys coming every Sunday, so you are doing a great job."

"Please, let me introduce to you my good friend Anita Fawun-Edoh. She assisted me today," Kika said, gently pushing Anita towards Madame Pat.

"Good Afternoon, madame, Caleb is beautiful, and what you are doing is truly great - I feel like we really connected today."

"Well, if you're not too busy during the week, perhaps you can come and help out at the orphanage, and have the chance to spend some more time with him?"

"Oh, I would love that!" Anita exclaimed. She knew that doing something positive with her day is just what she needed.

A journal to the reader

Dear Reader,

As a Christian, I believe everybody is put on this earth for one purpose. That purpose is to glorify God and spread his name across the universe. I also believe that for each person, there is more than one avenue to achieve this. This is what I call your YSP 'Your Specific Purpose'.

Most people feel this can only be linked to your career or your talents. In reality, it could be anything - from your experiences; to things that you enjoy doing; to your God-given personality. Whether you are a loud or quiet person, it is all for a reason.

As we spoke in previous journals, God's hand is always on your life. Meaning that, wherever you go or whatever you find yourself doing, it is orchestrated by the Holy Spirit. For example, being in the right place at the right time to meet the love of your life.

I will also add that everyone is given the power of choice. If you choose to do something or go somewhere that you know God is not a part of, there is a high chance that it may not go the way you had hoped. But God is so faithful that if you come back to him, he will let you in, put you back on the right track and use the old experiences you may probably not be proud of, to fulfil a purpose in your life.

I remember when I was looking for universities to go to after I pretty much had failed my first year of A-levels. I had grown up and was surrounded by people that will judge you based on what university you attend. So as I was applying, I would sign up for all these courses at top universities that, in hindsight, had nothing to do with what God wanted for me and had just the merest bit to do with the subjects I was studying at A levels. e.g. Product Design or Design Management. I got offers from three universities, and one of them had a course similar to what I loved, Architecture Design & Technology. However, it was not one of the top Universities, so I rejected their offer.

Results day came, and I ended up having to go through the Clearing Process. I actually had to call up the university I rejected to beg them for a place. They even made a joke about how I rejected them - it was quite funny!

Now looking back, I was always meant to do that course and go to that university. The course provided a smooth transition to Interior Design, which is what I do now, and that I absolutely love. This is a prime example of how I allowed other people's opinions to divert me away from what I was meant to do. But God is so good, he humbled me and put me back on track.

Can I just add that I ended up loving the university I went to, met some of my best friends there, and achieved a First Class Degree.

God is good!

Are there things you are doing at the moment that you feel is not for you? Would you honestly rather be doing something else?

I can tell you that if the passion is there, I believe it is part of God's plan for your life. He is the one that puts the passion in you. You may not know how he is going to use it, but you will find out one day.

Journal Task 9: Write down a list of everything you feel comes naturally to you (Your Specific Purpose). As mentioned, it could be talents, career, personality, experiences, passion. Once you have written a list, ask God what he wants you to do with each of them. You may not know now, but you will.

Tip: If you feel you have gone down the wrong path, do not feel it is ever too late. God is faithful. You just need to come back to him. Read the story of the Prodigal son. (Luke 15:11-33)

Lots of Love X

Simi Alexis Romeo

CHAPTER TEN

Tara

"Ow, Tara! Be careful!" Dabira screamed as Tara accidentally poked her with one of her fabric pins.

"I am sorry, I just really want to get this outfit to fit perfectly." This was the second time Tara was doing a dress fitting on Dabira. She felt she had done everything perfectly the first time, so she was confused as to why it did not fit right.

"Dabira, have you gained weight?" Tara asked cheekily.

"Oh my goodness, I am seriously going to slap you, how rude!" Dabira jokingly smacked Tara on the shoulder.

"I am sorry, but this dress is tight and last time I did a fitting, you were a perfect fit?" Tara laughed.

"Well, my weight fluctuates, and I usually get bloated around, and during my time of the month, it is not a big deal."

"It is a big deal considering the fact I am planning to do a photoshoot?" Tara said, rolling her eyes.

Once the ladies had completed the fitting session, Tara sat down and began to stare into the distance. "I need this fashion line to be successful," she muttered under her breath. It was said quietly but was loud enough for Dabira to hear.

"Aww, it will be Tara. You have worked so hard, and you are so talented."

She looked at Dabira, "Thanks, sis, I just feel that Bode is going through such a tough time. I need to step up my game and bring in some money too."

Tara's phone began to ring. When she saw who was calling, she hissed and threw her phone on the sofa.

"Why aren't you picking up Anita's calls?" Dabira asked, concerned.

"I just feel she wants to talk about the Bode and Rayo thing, and I know Anita; she wants to gloat and make me feel bad," Tara said, nervously folding her sample dresses to distract herself from the conversation.

"Well, Tara, if this is what you truly think of your best friend, there is a serious issue here. She should not want to see your downfall."

"No, I mean, she probably is coming from a good place, but the conversation will remind me how her life is perfect, and mine isn't, especially now that she is pregnant."

"Meaning?"

"Well, now she has gotten everything she has ever wished for - her life is perfect!"

Dabira sighed, "You don't know that! You never know what people are going through."

"Trust me, Dabira, she is living her best life. I can assure you."

Dabira shook her head. She did not understand why Tara always felt that everybody was better than her. She felt Tara still had a lot to work on and needed to be confident in her own story.

"Tara, do you know that there is one of you?"

Tara looked at Dabira, puzzled. "Well, last time I checked, I did not have a twin," she joked.

"Even if you were a twin, there would still be only one of you, and there has only ever been one of you, and there will only ever be one of you."

Tara could not see where Dabira was going with this, but she nodded.

"Okay, think about it, our fingerprints are all unique, one of a kind. Your past and life experiences are unique and one of a kind. And how you even look is unique and one of a kind."

"Dabira, I really do not have time for this, what's your point?"

"What I am saying is Anita's life is Anita's life; your life is your life. Don't waste your years thinking about others and what they are doing because believe me, you don't know the whole of their story."

Dabira was right. Tara was not aware of the struggles Anita was currently dealing with. Anita did not have the time or inclination to revel in the gossip around town when she had just lost her unborn child and husband. All she wanted to do was to speak to Tara and tell her what was going on. Tara, however, was too focused on herself and how her problems were greater than other people's, and therefore unable to even conceive that everyone does have their own fair share of issues.

"What are you reading?" Bode said as he entered the living room and saw Tara curled up on the sofa with a book.

"It's called, 'How far can you sew?' A book about becoming a fashion house and a million-dollar company."

Bode was impressed by how much energy Tara was putting into her business. He was even more impressed by how much she had stepped up since they lost their money. He would have thought Tara would be in a state of constant panic about the whole situation.

"So, how have your sessions with Pastor Lade been working out for you?" Bode asked.

"Well, I am actually trying to avoid her again," Tara said, disappointed in herself.

"What!? But why?" Bode was truly confused as Tara had appeared overjoyed after the first session with Pastor Lade and seemed to be embracing the 'therapy' whole-heartedly.

"Well, she wants me to do something that I'm not entirely comfortable with."

"Which is…?"

Tara paused for a few seconds before bringing up to courage to say, "She wants me to reach out to my mother."

Bode's eyes widened, he was aware that Tara and her mother did not have a great relationship, and that Tara had been brought up by her aunty. However, Tara never went into full details about it and also rarely spoke about her mother. He was amazed that Pastor Lade had been able to get Tara to the point where she not only talked about her mother, but was also being encouraged to reach out.

"Pastor Lade believes that I have not forgiven her for all the pain she caused me, which has brought me to a place where I'm carrying my apparent 'abandonment issues' to new situations and relationships." Tara said, aware that this was the first time she was about to open up to Bode about her mother being raped.

"So, if you don't mind me asking again, why do you and your mother not have a relationship," he asked, treading carefully.

"Well, my mum was raped by her teacher at 16, and out pops Tara," she said, trying to make light of the situation.

"Oh really? Wow!" Bode said in shock.

"Yep! Pastor Lade also feels my mum has not forgiven the guy that hurt her, hence why she sees me as 'pain'. So, she told me to invite her to a session. To be honest, I see where she is coming from."

Bode could see where she was coming from too, "I love you, babe, I am so happy your mother kept you. If anything, God needed you to be here for me."

Tara blushed, Bode always knew the right things to say.

"So what's the plan, are you going to reach out?" He said, trying not to push her.

"I don't know Bode. I honestly do not know what she is going to say when I do call her."

"Well, why don't we try now - together?" Bode knew how to make Tara feel comfortable. He never failed to show her how supportive he was in every situation.

"Well, what do I say?" Tara asked frantically.

"Maybe, we should invite her for lunch this weekend. At least that will allow us time to speak, and, in the process, we'll invite her to the therapy sessions with Pastor Lade?"

Tara reluctantly picked up her phone and began to scroll through her contact list. Bode put his arm around her the whole time, giving her the emotional support she needed. Suddenly she came across her mother's name and number. "Okay, here it goes…"

The phone began to ring.

"Hello."

"Hi mum. Erm, it's me, Tara."

There was a long pause.

"Oh, hello."

Tara began to feel increasingly uncomfortable.

"Well, I don't know if you heard, but I am engaged to be married and um, well, my fiancé would love to meet you. How do you feel about that?"

"Well, that's nice. Congratulations." What she said was great, but Tara could not understand why it felt so cold.

"Thank you. So, would you like to come and visit this Saturday at around 1:30 pm?" Tara asked awkwardly.

There was another long pause. Tara could feel her heart pounding out of her chest. She was shaking as she waited for her mother's response.

"Sure. Text me the details. I have to run."

Before Tara could respond, her mother had ended the call. She looked at Bode, unsure whether that went well or not.

"Well, she said yes! That's good, isn't it?" Bode assured her.

"But did she want to say yes?" Tara felt that her mother was trying to get her off the phone as quickly as possible and therefore said whatever she thought was necessary to make Tara leave her alone.

"Don't doubt it, Tara, she said yes. I think you should text her the details, tell her you are excited to see her, and we'll leave everything else in God's hands. It's all going to work out." He said, kissing her on the forehead.

Tara tried to force herself to ignore her negative thoughts and see just the positive. Bode was probably right. She was very likely reading too much into it. The conversation was bound to be awkward because they do have an awkward relationship.

She quickly sent her mother a text message with the

date, time, and address. She followed the text with a call to Pastor Lade, to keep her in the loop.

Kika

It was Saturday morning, and Kika was ecstatic that her weekend was just beginning. The last few days at work had been extremely awkward. Ms Gozy would not even acknowledge her just because she refused to give her the dirt on Mimi and Tara. She was a hundred percent sure that if Miss Gozy did not get over that disappointment soon, she would be fired. The only thing she had going for her was her stationery brand. As well as the 'Cards of Courage', Kika had also designed Journals, Fountain Pens, and Diaries. She had not shown any of her friends her collection besides the cards, but she was pretty sure that it will also have a positive impact on them.

Kika felt it would be nice to stop by at Tara's to give her a gift bag filled with the collection because of the rough time she had been going through. She was looking forward to seeing her hopefully, excited reaction.

On her way, she received a phone call from Mimi.

"Hey Mimi, how are you?" Kika said excitedly.

"I am good, girl! What are you up to?" Mimi asked.

"I am on my way to Tara's house to drop off a gift bag of my stationery collection."

"Oh," Mimi said jittery, still unsure where her friendship with Tara stood.

"Is everything okay?" Kika said, noticing the apprehensiveness in Mimi's voice.

"Yes, everything is fine. Have you spoken to Anita?" Mimi said, trying to change the subject.

Kika had not seen much of Anita over the last week. Every day, Anita would wake up early and head to the orphanage. Kika could see how Anita's life was changing positively. She seemed a lot happier, and it reminded her of their days in university.

"Not recently," Kika tried her best not to lie.

"Well, I don't know if you have seen it, but I interviewed with 'The Roma Show' on the whole situation with Rayo." Mimi confessed, but quickly changed the subject, "I am having a celebratory dinner to celebrate being free, as it was so difficult to speak about the subject."

Kika was confused. She had not heard anything about the interview, and if Mimi had chosen to go with 'The Roma Show', a competitor media outlet, that will only make Ms Gozy even more furious.

"When did the interview come out?" Kika asked.

"It came out about half an hour ago - I thought you would have seen it since it is your industry," Mimi nervously joked.

Kika was furious. She understood what Mimi was going through was horrible, but why did she not think that maybe she could have helped her out by interviewing with 'Hello Lagos' instead.

"I am inviting all the girls plus my lawyer Dami. It is, however, awkward because Tara can't make it, and Anita is not picking up," Mimi continued.

Kika remained silent on the phone.

"Hello? Kika, are you there?"

"Why am I always forgotten about?"

"What do you mean?" Mimi asked, pretending to be completely oblivious to the fact that her actions had hurt Kika's feelings.

"Mimi, I asked you whether 'Hello Lagos' could interview you, and you were so adamant that you did not want to do that. Now, you are saying that you have gone with

'The Roma Show', our competitor? How do you think this will make me look?'"

Mimi sighed, "Kika when you asked me, I was honest. I did not want to do anything like that, because of my fear that Rayo will come after me. However, my lawyer insisted that it might help lure Rayo out of his hiding place. He organised this and said, 'The Roma Show' is the most genuine outlet; they would not twist my words. And because this is such a huge deal, I needed it to be my words. 'Hello Lagos' is known for twisting words!"

Kika was readily able to acknowledge that 'Hello Lagos' is somewhat messy, but why would Mimi not trust that she would ensure her words will be used correctly.

"Did you not feel that I could take care of you?" Kika eventually asked.

Mimi giggled, "Kika you cannot even stand up to Ms Gozy for yourself, what makes you think I would trust that you would be able to stand up to her for me?"

Instantly Kika went to a place she had not been for a while. She went to a place where she felt dismissed, a place where she was not taken seriously by others, where she felt belittled. She was hurt, and her anger got the better of her.

"I will have you know that Ms Gozy offered me a huge promotion, N1 million salary increase, higher position, writing my own segment, all of that just to throw YOU under the bus, and I turned it all down because I valued our friendship. Now she pretty much hates me and is probably going to fire me, especially now that this interview has come out. So, don't you dare tell me that I am unable to stand up for myself, because when it mattered, I did!" She yelled.

Mimi paused.

"Okay, Kika, please don't make this about yourself. I am going through a life and death situation that concerns me, my sons, my family, and my business. I did what was best for me. I understand you are hurt - but you are worth more than Ms Gozy. Go and start your own blog, work on this stationery collection, and while you are at it, why don't you read your own cards?" Mimi said, irritated. "Look, I hope you can come to my celebratory dinner and support me in my struggle. I love you. Bye."

Mimi had put down the phone. This was very typical of her; she hated conflict and was very quick to brush anything under the carpet. Without a doubt, Kika knew she would be attending the dinner, but she could not help but be apprehensive about the coming furious reaction from Ms Gozy. She was petrified.

On arriving at Tara's, Kika was too upset to meet up with her. So she dropped off the gift bag with her security guard to take in. On her way back home, she began to cry. She did not want to lose her job; she felt she had a lot more growing to do at 'Hello Lagos'. She wanted to make a name for herself there.

But out of nowhere, she suddenly felt an overflow of peace and calmness wash over her. In her heart, she felt the words come to her:

"For I know the plans I have for you," declares the Lord, "plans to prosper you and not to harm you, plans to give you hope and a future." - Jeremiah 29:11.

No matter what happens, Kika knew she would be fine as she had God's hand on her life.

She put on some praise and worship music to lift her spirits, but just as the beat was about to drop, a phone call came through from Ms Gozy.

Kika gulped, "Hello,"

"Kika, I am sure you know why I am pissed!" Ms Gozy said furiously.

Kika sighed, "Yes ma, Mimi did not want to interview with us, unfortunately. Her lawyer made her go with 'The Roma Show'."

"Kika, I honestly do not know why I have kept you for so long? You are useless, worthless, and pretty much a waste of space. What is the use of you, please tell me?" Ms Gozy said in anger.

Labels - this was something Kika had gone through when she was younger. People telling you what you are and not what you believe you are. Not what God says about you. God says in his word that she is his prized possession; she is fearfully and wonderfully made; and that she is valued. Why would this woman have the audacity to say otherwise?

Kika felt a sense of strength.

"Ms Gozy, with all due respect, I am not useless. I am a good person with a heart. Mimi is going through something life-shattering; she did not trust 'Hello Lagos' to carry her story because of what we may twist. Maybe as a business, we need to look at changing our approach so that people can trust us more."

Ms Gozy laughed, "Are you really trying to teach me about a business I have built from the ground up? Seriously?"

"I am just making a suggestion for the future?" Kika said boldly.

"Kika, you are fired. I am done with you!" Ms Gozy cut the call.

Kika froze. She had tried to anticipate the various emotions she might feel when she heard those words. Nothing, Kika felt nothing.

Anita

Anita had been going to the orphanage daily to spend time with Caleb. She helped him with his homework and played games with him and the other children. Every night when she went back home to Kika's house, she felt more and more fulfilled. She continued attending mid-week services and had even begun the Sunday services, as well. This was the happiest she had been in a long time - she was in her prime.

Anita was home alone in the kitchen, making her favourite, green tea with Manuka honey when her phone rang. She looked at her screen and saw a random number. She had kept her distance from all her friends and social media and had no idea what was going on in anyone's life. She wanted to go through this tough time on her own and ensure she was in a good place before letting others know.

"That's strange," she thought to herself. She did not like to pick up calls from random numbers, so she put her phone down just as the kettle finished boiling. She picked up the kettle and gently poured the hot water into her mug. At that point, her phone rang again. She rolled her eyes, and reluctantly picked it up. 'If they called you twice - it must be important', was her motto.

"Hello," Anita said irritably.

"Hey, it's me."

Anita had chills down her spine as soon as she heard the voice on the other end of the line. Her heart started beating extremely fast, and she had lost the ability to speak. She had not heard Nati's voice for months as she ensured she avoided him at all costs.

"Please, don't hang up!" he said quickly.

Once she caught her breath, she nervously coughed, "what do you want, Nati?"

"Anita, I could never apologise to you enough - "

"I don't want to hear it," she stopped him.

Nati sighed, "Please, Anita, can we please see each other. I know what I did; there is probably no coming back from this. But I just need to talk to you. These last few months without you have been absolute hell."

Anita closed her eyes. She was incredibly stressed out about all that Nati had put her through and did not feel he deserved any of her time. As she opened her eyelids, her eyes began to sting and well up. She tried to hold back the tears, but without fail, they slowly began to fall.

"Do you feel like you deserve time to talk to me?" Anita questioned.

"No, I do not. This is the reason I am begging for your time." Nati reasoned.

Anita's stomach began to turn; she felt sick. How on earth was she the one going through this? She took a large gulp and reluctantly agreed to meet Nati at their home.

"Thank you, baby; I am excited for you to come home."

Anita dropped the phone irritated that Nati still felt entitled to call her pet names. Kika had gone out to run some errands, so she felt incredibly lost and uncomfortable. Times like this, she would be seeking Kika's advice. Was she making the right decision to go and see Nati? Was her mind in the right place? What if she could not resist Nati and his charm.

"I'll just call her," Anita thought to herself.

She picked up her phone and scrolled down to Kika's number and dialled.

Kika's phone went straight to voicemail.

"She is probably busy; I will just send her a message," Anita thought to herself.

[Hey girl, when are you back? I need to talk to you urgently - call me when you can.]

Anita sat down on the sofa, exasperated. She needed Kika to help her through this. She was the only person she felt she could truly rely on. She definitely couldn't trust her own judgement at this time.

The longer it took for Kika to respond to her message, the more restless Anita became. She kept walking up and down the living room, scrolling through her contacts, tempted to maybe speak to one of the other girls. "They have no idea what is even going on," she said to herself. Anita was so restless, she began searching for advice on YouTube, but nothing felt right.

And then she remembered:

"Trust in the Lord with all your heart and lean not on your own understanding; in all your ways submit to him and he will direct your paths." Proverbs 3: 5-6.

"Hmm, I guess I am not supposed to know the answers. I am supposed to trust in God?" Anita felt that she still needed Kika to confirm this thought. She knew the passage said she should trust in God, but she did not know much about him. Sure, she had been attending church, but she still had not done anything on her own. How can she trust in what she has no understanding of whatsoever?

Her phone started to ring.

"Kika, I have been anxiously waiting for you to get back to me," Anita shrieked.

"I'm so sorry Ani, I am in a bit of a situation. What's up?" Kika responded.

"Nati called me. He wants us to meet up - what do you

think I should do?" Anita said oblivious to the fact Kika herself was not in the best of moods.

"Really, he called, and you answered?" Kika asked, confused.

"Yes. Well, it was with a private number. If I had known it was him, I would not have answered it." She said, defending her decision.

Kika sighed.

Anita noticed Kika wasn't herself; it felt like she was slightly irritated.

"Is everything okay, love?" She asked.

"Yes sorry, I just have a lot on my mind. Look, Anita, follow your heart, no answer is wrong. Just be careful. Your decision determines your destiny. Think about how you want this to end." Kika said.

"I am not sure, what do you think?" Anita asked.

Kika tried to hide her frustration. "Pray to God Ani, he will direct you."

"But I don't have that relationship."

"You do! Just speak to him. I am so sorry, but I have to run. I will call you back once I finish sorting this out, okay? I love you."

Before Anita could respond, the call had ended.

She put the phone down on the side table and buried her head into the palm of her hands. It was at this point she realised she had become that 'needy friend'. The one that just 'takes' and never 'gives'. When she and Kika were growing up, she was always the one Kika needed. She remembered how infuriating she found it at times. Until Kika began to take her relationship with God a lot more seriously, she started relying on God a lot more.

Maybe this is what she needed. Perhaps she needed to start trusting in God.

She went to her bedroom, knelt at the edge of her bed,

put her hands together, and closed her eyes. At least that is what she remembers from Sunday school and what she sees others doing during service at church.

"Dear God" she sighed, "this is hard for me to do. Obviously, the last few months have been up and down, incredibly painful, yet fulfilling," Anita started to weep.

She took her mind back to when she first discovered she was pregnant, how she was so happy that her prayers had been answered. She remembered the moment she overheard Nati on the phone and then finding out about his affair, and how she felt her life had ended. Then finally, she remembered how she took that bold step of going to church, connecting with baby Caleb from the orphanage and, how it had all brought purpose to her life. At that moment, she thought to herself that maybe she was meant to be going through this. Maybe, it was part of her journey to discovering her purpose. In fellowship, Ola would always say that God is in control of everything - the good, the bad, and the ugly and how everything does happen for a reason - but Anita just could not understand this.

"Lord, if you are real, why did this happen?!" She screamed. "Why couldn't I have a baby all those years, and when I finally got pregnant, why would you take the baby away! Why would you give another woman MY baby." She dropped on the floor, curled herself into a foetal position, and cried hysterically. Although Anita was angry at God, she knew she felt a presence, and she knew it only meant one thing, God was most definitely real.

A journal to the reader

Dear Reader,

I love how God equips you in life. Pastor Lade had advised Tara to reach out to her mother, and she was dreading it. Luckily, she has the perfect person in her life, Bode, to help her embark on this journey.

You may find yourself in a position where you would like to start something or do something new. It could be starting a business, traveling the world, or even learning a new skill. However, you feel you can't do it because you may not have enough funds or time or have the right connections to achieve it. So, you park the idea and postpone it for the future, which may never come.

If it is God's plan for your life and part of your purpose, he will equip you with the funding, the time, and the connections to fulfil that purpose.

Same goes for when you go through hard times; God has equipped you with his word (The Bible) and strength to overcome it. Those hard times are part of your purpose, perhaps to help other people who may go through similar trials in the future.

Hebrews 2:18: "For because he himself has suffered when tempted, he is able to help those who are being tempted".

When I started my children's charity, Happy Kids - Promising Purpose, a charity that supports underprivileged children in Nigeria, I was absolutely petrified. The intent was to throw this huge Christmas party, where we hire out a venue with rides and give the kids free food, presents, etc. The first time I did it was so scary, because I personally could not afford it and I was also scared of failure. I did not live in Nigeria and had only a few friends there, so I did not feel I would have as much support. I also was not comfortable asking people for donations. It was so awkward.

However, I realised that this had nothing to do with me and everything to do with the children. I cringed as I sent every message begging people for donations and sending email after email for sponsorship.

It was amazing to see how God moved. A lot of my friends and family made my vision their priority and did everything they could to help. Organisations and businesses I did not expect became sponsors. I was introduced to an event planner who handled everything from Nigeria and gave me a massive discount. A lot of people I did not expect gave generous donations.

The positive thing that came from the whole experience was that my faith levels increased.

Journal Task 10: Make a spider diagram of each gift you put on the list in journal 9. On the spider's legs, write down everything you feel can come from this particular gift and what you need to achieve it. Then say this prayer.

Dear God, I thank you for all the gifts you have given me. I pray that everything you put in me will be utilised for the purpose of your kingdom. Like the Bible story of the talents (Matthew 25:14–30), I pray I will nurture those talents, and it will be multiplied, direct me on how you would like me to achieve it. Thank you, Lord. Amen!

Tip: Philippians 1:6 "…He who began a good work in you will carry it on to completion until the day of Christ Jesus."

Lots of Love X

Simi Alexis Romeo

CHAPTER ELEVEN

Anita

Anita gently smacked her lips while dabbing at the corners of her mouth to ensure none of her lip gloss had smudged out of her lip line. She smiled at herself in the mirror and nodded, "you can do this, Anita." She took her phone out and ordered her Uber.

"Five minutes away," she whispered.

She scurried nervously around the flat, looking for her handbag so she would be ready to go once the taxi arrived. She did not know where this conversation with Nati was going to go. She was hopeful that they would reconcile their issues, but at the same time, she wasn't ready to accept someone else's baby.

A notification came up on her phone: [your driver has arrived]

Anita walked out of Kika's house, located her driver, and got into the car.

"Hi, good afternoon."

"Hi, madame, where am I taking you this fine

morning?"

"I'm going home." Anita tensed her face in fear of what was to come. She bent her head down and anxiously scrolled through her phone. She was not only uncomfortable about seeing Nati, but she was also trying to avoid a chatty taxi driver.

A few minutes later, the driver pulled up to her gated fence, Anita's stomach started to turn. She got out of the car and knocked on the gate. James, her trusted gateman, came out of the security post. His eyes lit up when he saw her.

"Madame, Oga said you had travelled." Oga is a term used in Nigerian lingo for a male boss, "usually when you travel, you tell me and give me something." James continued in hope.

Something meaning money, Anita rolled her eyes, "James, I am coming. Let me get into the house and sit down first." A begging gateman was not something she could be bothered to deal with at the moment.

As she rummaged through her handbag for her house keys, she was startled by the sudden opening of the front door.

"Beautiful, I have missed you!" Nati said earnestly.

He looked down at Anita with his gorgeous brown eyes. He was wearing a crisp white shirt with a navy-blue blazer and blue jeans. He looked good, he smelt good as usual, and Anita was worried she would not be able to resist his entreaties.

She looked back into his eyes. She had truly missed him, but she knew that this visit could not be all fun and games. This was the point where they needed to decide how they were going to move forward - with or without each other? If they stayed together, would they embrace this child as their own, or will she be having 'baby mama' issues? That was the central issue for Anita, and one which made her uncertain about the future and how they would cope.

"Babe, I have missed you!" Nati said again while putting his arms around her. Anita felt very warm in his arms. She felt herself desiring to lay her head on his chest as he kissed her forehead, which usually happened when they hadn't seen each other in a long while. She forced herself to snap out of the reverie. Getting into old habits is not what was going to salvage their relationship.

"I missed you too Nati, shall we go inside?"

He stood back and watched Anita as she walked into their front living room. He was in awe as she sat down on their three-seater sofa.

"What?" She sniggered as she caught his gaze.

"Would you like some green tea?" he asked, knowing that was her favourite drink and a way to ease the awkwardness.

She smiled, "yes, please."

He went to the kitchen and told the cook to prepare some tea, fried rice, and peppered chicken. He knew this was the way to Anita's heart.

"Is your mother here?" She asked, hoping she wasn't.

"Oh no, I have not seen my mother since the day at the hospital."

"What!? That was months ago?"

"I hated how she spoke to you and made you feel Anita," he said remorsefully. "After everything that I put you through, you did not deserve to be disrespected."

"But Nati, that does not mean you should not speak to her. She loves you and wants the best for you."

Anita was shocked that Nati was taking her side for once. Nati's mother could do no wrong in his eyes. He was the epitome of a 'mummy's boy' and his mother was his angel. That night at the hospital was not the first time Nati's mother had spoken to or about her in a derogatory manner. She had a feeling that it must be because Nati himself felt so guilty that he was the cause of the problem.

"My mum would be okay; what I need to sort out is you and me. Babe, I am so, so sorry. I cannot be more sorry."

"The thing is Nati, I have forgiven you, but my fear is, can I ever trust you again? Will I be okay with your child and this 'D' lady? Will I ever become a mother myself? it has been a lot to deal with."

"Well, I hope I put your mind to rest when I tell you that the 'D' lady has decided not to keep the baby."

Anita's eyes widened.

"Yes, I was shocked too at her decision, considering I had been pleading with her all along that I did not want the baby. I related everything that had happened between us to her, and I think she felt guilty. She called me a couple of days ago to tell me she was getting rid of the baby, and she wants nothing more to do with me. I feel the same way, so I could not be more relieved." He said, reaching out to hold Anita's hand.

Anita pulled away. She was relieved, too, but was still baffled about everything.

"Is getting rid of the baby the right thing to do, though, Nati?" She asked.

"Anita, it is a blessing in disguise, that baby will forever be a reminder of how I hurt you. Now we can move on and work on us." He leaned towards her and kissed her forehead. "I am so mad at myself for hurting you, please move back home. I promise this will never happen again."

A lot was going through Anita's mind. On the one hand, she was incredibly thrilled that she and Nati are now able to move forward - they can work on their relationship and maybe continue trying for a baby. On the other hand, should D get rid of the baby? They had tried for a baby for many years, but it never happened for them. Meanwhile, it has happened for Nati, and just because it wasn't in their preferred scenario, would killing a child to erase the past, be the right thing to do?

She shook her head, trying to ignore her thoughts. D choosing to have an abortion had to be a sign from God. He knew she could not handle the infidelity continually being thrown in her face if the child existed.

"Okay!" she smiled. "Tomorrow, I will get the rest of my stuff from Kika's." Anita wondered whether she had let him off too easily, but she felt she was over it. She felt she was ready to be Mrs Edoh again. She believed Nati deeply regretted his actions.

That night, as she laid her head on her duck feathered pillows that she had missed so much, Anita was unable to sleep. All she could think of was how it was so unfair to kill a child, especially as she had desired one for so long, and how she had even connected with Caleb over the last few months. She felt a sense of guilt that she was allowing D to go through with this.

She rolled out of her bed and went downstairs to the kitchen to make herself some tea. As the kettle was simmering to a boiling point, Anita picked it up to carefully pour the hot water into her grey mug and place it on the worktop to cool. She turned around, leant over the kitchen counter, and buried her face in her hands.

"God, what do I do? I need your guidance," she frantically expressed. She then suddenly felt an overflow of calmness and peace. In her heart, she knew what she had to do. Tomorrow morning, she was going to ask Nati for D's number. She needed to call her and tell her not to get rid of the baby. This was an incredibly difficult decision, but although that child was not hers, she already felt love for them, being a piece of her husband, Nati, whom she loved very much. And as it was Nati's selfish actions that caused this, that child was not at fault and deserved to live and be loved. She felt that if D did choose to keep the baby, all three of them would go through counselling and work it all out.

She finished her tea and went back to bed.

Anita was extremely proud of who she was becoming. Growing up, she never would decide anything for herself. Her whole life had been planned out for her by her parents. From what subjects she was going to study at school, to the kind of woman she was going to be. And when she met her husband in university, she merely transferred the responsibility over to him and relied on Nati solely for every decision she needed to make. But when things broke down in her marriage, she found she only had Kika to rely on for support, and it was Kika who taught her how she needed to rely on God.

She was excited to have made the decision to contact D in the morning. She knew it was daring, but she knew it was the right thing to do. At the end of the day, she felt strong. She was strong enough to accept D's baby, and she knew that this was growth.

The morning swiftly came, and Anita's excitement to contact D had taken a drastic turn. She retracted everything she felt from the previous night and decided she could not do it. She was fearful. She also did not have D's number and did not want to ask Nati for it. Anita also thought about the possible effects of it on her marriage to Nati - how did he actually feel about this woman? There were so many questions that remain unanswered.

Nati woke up shortly after and noticed the worried look on his wife's face.

"Is everything alright, dear?" he asked, "you haven't changed your mind about staying here, have you?"

Anita smiled. "Good morning, my love. Everything is fine. I just have a lot on my mind."

Nati moved closer to Anita; he knew this was not going to be smooth sailing, even as she had agreed to move back home. He knew that it was going to take a lot for his wife to trust him again. He gently stroked her cheek and looked into her eyes.

"Babe, I just want to say thank you for your forgiveness. I know what I did was wrong and disrespectful on so many levels, and I am grateful for your forgiveness."

Nati leaned in to kiss his wife. Anita smiled and returned the kiss. She did not want their relationship to go sour, and if D had decided to get rid of the baby, maybe that is God's blessing to her and Nati's relationship, and now they can move on.

"I need to go to Kika's to pick up the rest of my stuff, will you go with me?"

"Why, of course." Nati grinned.

Kika was in absolute shock when she saw Nati and Anita laughing with each other at her front door.

"So, everything is all good here?" Kika asked, confused.

Nati laughed, "Thank you for being my wife's rock

when I failed as a husband, Kika. It is wonderful that Anita has good friends like you to be by her side."

Kika blinked rapidly while nodding her head. "That's absolutely fine, Nati." She turned to Anita, "Ani, let's go get the rest of your stuff from the bedroom. I also have some more 'Cards of Courage' to give you before you leave, especially since you have now made such a huge decision," She said, judging the situation.

"Yes, sure!" Anita said excitedly. She loved Kika's cards. They helped motivate her and were helping to shape her into someone she was proud of. She followed Kika to the bedroom and began to put her things into her suitcase.

Kika felt extremely uncomfortable that Anita and Nati were back together so quickly. It had been a painful experience, and she felt that they had just jumped back into their relationship without examining the core issues responsible for the split, and the best way to rebuild the trust.

"So, what happened? I thought you and Nati were going to discuss how you were going to get back together or move on, not actually get together. I am quite surprised at how everything has suddenly gone back to normal from one conversation," Kika said, carefully watching her words to try to ensure she does not come across as judgemental.

"I forgave him!" said Anita, "he has apologised and treated me like an absolute diamond since."

"What, since yesterday?" Kika said under her breath, causing Anita to look up at her.

"Did you say something?" Anita asked.

"Anita, he treated you like an absolute diamond while he was cheating on you and having babies with other women." Kika blurted out. She was notorious for being controlling and telling people how they should live their lives. She knew this was a flaw of hers, but she wanted the best for Anita, and could not help it. She felt she could not watch her best friend go back to a time of pain in her life without speaking out. She would never forgive herself.

Anita looked at Kika with disapproval. "So what, you expect me not to forgive my husband? That's not very Christian, Kika. Plus, there is no baby - D has decided to get rid of it."

"Anita, forgiveness, and being Christian does not mean you should not value yourself and your worth. He broke your heart, your trust, and you - he put you through a lot. I do expect you to forgive him, but I feel maybe it should take time, and both of you should go through Christian counselling. Remember that you did not suspect anything before, you can't go back into this relationship blindly," Kika pleaded. "And what about Caleb and church, are you now just going to go back to your old ways?"

Anita felt extremely judged by Kika.

She looked her dead in the eyes. "You wouldn't understand, you're not married!" Anita said without an inch of emotion. "I enjoyed my time in church and with Caleb, but I need to go back to MY marriage - okay? When you eventually find a man, then you can call me."

Kika looked at her in disbelief. Anita was very much aware of how Kika struggled with being single in her late 20s and feeling less than her peers because of it. Kika felt it was an extremely low blow by Anita when all she desired was the best for her.

"I guess I wouldn't understand," Kika said solemnly, as she handed her the cards. "Well, I pray that everything works out for you and Nati."

"It will!" Anita took the cards, grabbed her suitcase, and took it to the living room.

"Let's get out of this negative environment now, Nati!" Anita walked out of the front door before Nati could even question her.

He looked over at Kika, confused, who was standing at the entrance of the corridor.

She shrugged.

"Bye, Kika, thanks for everything," Nati said.

She smiled and waved goodbye.

She went upstairs to her bedroom and wept.

Tara

"Where is she, Bode? it's 1:35 pm!" Tara asked, walking up and down the dining room in distress. "She was meant to be here an hour ago."

"She is probably just running late. You know - 'African Time'?" Bode said, trying to calm her down, "have you called her?"

"Yes, I have literally been calling all morning, but her phone is going to voicemail." Tara picked up her phone and gave it to Bode. "Why don't you try?"

"What is going on here?" Dabira walked in, interrupting their frantic episode. She was quickly distracted by the beautiful food that had been laid out on the table. "I honestly do not understand why, but I am seriously so hungry. Can I have a-"

"No! It's for my mother, Dabira," Tara yelled.

"Your mother, as in aunty Tola?" Dabira asked.

"Yes!"

"Your mum is in London with my mum, I just spoke to them this morning," Dabira said confused.

"No, that cannot be right, because she'd agreed to have lunch with us this afternoon?" Bode said agitatedly.

"Trust me! Why did you not tell me you planned this lunch, I would have warned you. You know your mum can be funny?" Dabira said, trying to ease the tension.

Tara was heartbroken. She had hoped to mend all her

issues with her mum, and now she could not believe she had gotten stood up.

"I am going to my room, don't follow me," she said solemnly. As she slowly dragged herself to the room, Bode and Dabira were both distraught when they began to hear Tara gasp for air and sniffle. They knew she was crying.

"Dabira, can I please have your mum's number, this is absurd and not fair." Bode said sternly.

"Absolutely, but honestly Bode, aunty Tola is a broken woman and has not allowed herself to heal from the pains of her past. It is why we all give her a pass."

"But Tara is suffering from all of this. Can you not see that?"

"I can, and I love Tara so much, so my heart bleeds for her. But her mother is also suffering. They both did nothing wrong to deserve the pain they are going through, and people deal with things differently. You have to be understanding of this.

Bode could see where Dabira was coming from, but his main concern was for his wife-to-be, Tara. He nodded and made his way to the study to give aunty Lola, Dabira's mother a call. Dabira stayed in the dining room and began to eat the lunch that had been prepared.

"Good afternoon, is this aunty Lola?"

"Hello, yes, it is. Who is speaking, please?"

"This is Bode, Tara's fiancé. How are you, ma?"

"Oh wow, finally, I get to speak to the guy that has swept our daughter off her feet. How are you, Mr Cole?"

"I am very well, thank you! I am calling to ask about aunty Tola, your sister. Tara and I had prepared lunch for her here this afternoon but were surprised to find out that she is in London. I am not sure if you knew about this, but Tara is weeping as we speak."

There was a long pause on the phone.

"Yes, she is in London with me. Sorry, I had no idea, please hold." Aunty Lola said.

As Bode was waiting for aunty Lola to come back, he noticed that she had not put him on hold and could over-hear the conversation she was having with her sister.

"Tola, you did not cancel your plans with them?" Aunty Lola screamed.

"I did not want all the begging and the pleading." Aunty Tola said, nonchalantly.

"But they had prepared for you and cooked etcetera. It is rude to not just show up, plus they probably spent good money preparing for this."

Aunty Tola laughed, "Well, I will send them a cheque, I hear they need money right now."

At that point, Bode had heard enough. He realised Tara's mother had no interest in pursuing or salvaging any form of relationship with Tara. The only thing he hoped is that Tara can heal from this without her mother's input. He dropped the phone and called Pastor Lade to tell her what had been happening.

"This is so painful to hear Bode, but she still has the power to get through this. She needs to forgive her mother, pray for her, and hope one day there will be some sort of relationship." Pastor Lade expressed.

"I think she can do this. Please can you give her a call in an hour or so?" Bode said, hopeful.

"Absolutely!"

Tara had cried herself to sleep and had done so for a few hours when she was awakened by her phone ringing. "Good afternoon Pastor Lade."

"Tara, did I wake you?" Pastor Lade asked.

"It's fine. I need to get up anyway. How are you?"

"I am well, thank you. Bode called me to tell me about what happened earlier."

"Yes, I tried and failed Pastor," Tara was convinced there was no hope for her and her mum. She couldn't help but wonder whether this would affect her for the rest of her life. It does take two to tango at the end of the day, and if her mother was not willing to tango with her, forgiveness is probably not on the cards. "I am officially going to be a mess for the rest of my life now."

"No, Tara, do not be a victim of other people's mistakes," Pastor Lade said passionately, "you need to work on forgiving your mum. Easier said than done, but just start by saying a prayer for her every day and asking the Lord to help you to forgive."

"Mmm…"

"And in the meantime, focus on yourself! Work on your fashion label like never before, be a good friend to those around you, and work on becoming a great wife to Bode. Continue to pray and put the effort in, and God will meet your needs. No doubt about that."

Tara felt a sense of comfort and motivation based on what Pastor Lade was saying.

"You are right Pastor, thank you so much for your encouraging words."

She got off the phone and began to pray.

"Dear God, I am thankful for the people you placed in my life. Bode, Aunty Lola and Dabira, my friends Anita, Kika and Mimi, and Pastor Lade. I am so blessed to have good people constantly around me. I pray for my mum. I pray she forgives me, and I forgive her. Heal our relationship. In Jesus' name. Amen."

At that point, Tara hurried out of bed, tripping on the gift bag that Kika dropped off a few days ago from her new stationery collection. The bag fell sideways, and all these impeccably designed stationery products spread across the bedroom floor. She bent down to put everything back, and one of the journals caught her attention. It was a gorgeous rose gold colour, with a Bible scripture written in embroidery saying,

"I can do ALL things through Christ who strengthens me - Philippians 4:13".

Tara began to look at the scripture and re-read it over and over again - was this meant for her? Was God trying to tell her something?

"I can do all things through Christ who strengthens me," she chanted slowly. "I, Omotara Williams - soon to be Cole can do all things through Christ who strengthens me." She said again. "This means that I can forgive my mum, I can forgive others, I can launch The Tara Cole Collection and be extremely successful, and make lots of money. I can do it all through Christ!"

Tara opened up the journal and began to plan how she intended to make her dreams come true. She thought about planning the most fantastic photoshoot and using all her friends as models to cut down on costs. Tara was ready - she was prepared, and nothing was going to stop her - nothing at all.

Kika

Kika lay on her bed, staring at the ceiling. She had to get ready for Mimi's celebratory dinner shortly, but she felt she was in a dark place, a pit. She had never felt so isolated and lonely. The last few weeks had been life-changing, and she was pretty unsure about where she was heading next. It had been a week since she lost her job at 'Hello Lagos'. Something she had worked so hard for, for eight years. It was disheartening that she lost it all due to Mimi's unfortunate situation. She was not sure what was next for her, career-wise. She had the stationery collection, but was that really going to pay her bills?

She was also not in the best place with Anita. Kika felt, as usual, she would go over and beyond for her friendships, but her friends would always choose others over her. She understood that Nati and Anita are husband and wife and that he ultimately does come first. But after the way Nati disrespected and hurt her, she thought that maybe Anita would treat her a bit better after she was there to pick up the pieces. It was not right that Anita would call her out on her 'singleness' and abandon her when all she was doing was to try to help.

This singleness issue was something Kika tried not to think about. She had always dreamt of being married in her early 20's. It was what she was told would happen from a young age. You go to school, then to university, find a job, and then you get married. It was that simple. Kika was pushing 30, and she did not even have a boyfriend. All her friends were married, and she gets constant pressure from her parents and society in general. It was not like she was not open to it, because she was; it just was not yet her time - which is what she tried to tell herself again and again.

Kika took out her journal and began to write a letter to God. She already knew about the appointed time; her own prayer was to be okay with it and not to feel inadequate like it was her fault. What made Anita, Mimi, and Tara so different from her?

At that moment, Kika received a text message from

Ola. She was the leader at her mid-week services in church.

[Hi Kika, you have been on my mind. Just wanted to check on you]

Kika looked at the message and thought to herself that it came at the perfect time. Kika was the type of person that wanted to be there for others but found it uncomfortable when others were there for her. She felt that she should not need to rely on people, only God. However, she felt Ola's text message was a sign from God.

She took the initiative and thought to call Ola and give her a breakdown of what she was going through.

"Wow, Kika, I cannot believe you have been dealing with all this alone. That is a lot for one person," Ola said kindly. "About Anita, it is sad because I know you want the best for her, but you have done your part. You were her rock at a horrific time in her life. She is a little defensive at the moment. Give her time and still be supportive of her decisions. That is what a good friend does."

"Yeah," Kika said. "I probably came across a little bit judgemental that she took Nati back so easily."

"Exactly, and that just put her on the defensive. Hence the reason why she retaliated nastily by bringing up the marriage thing," Ola continued.

Kika was happy that she had spoken to Ola. She helped put everything into perspective - iron indeed does sharpen iron.

"Oh, and Kika on the marriage thing, it sucks. I did not get married until I was 33. There is no reason behind it, and there is not a particular way to go about it. It all boils down to God's perfect timing."

"Mhmm." Kika was so bored about hearing over and over again about God's timing.

"Marriage is not all shiny. Look at your friends, Mimi

and Anita - are those the kind of marriages you want?" Ola asked.

"No way - the only relationship in our friendship group that seems legit is Tara and Bode. I have always felt uncomfortable about Mimi and Rayo. With Anita and Nati, he treated her well, but he was not encouraging of her and her dreams; he was too self-centred," Kika said.

"Exactly, and just because Tara and Bode seem great, does not mean it will always be great. I have been married for five years now. My husband was definitely worth the wait. However, there are times I want to chill by myself for the whole day and watch a movie. That cannot happen. I have a family to take care of. I am up at 6 am every morning; I have to get the kids ready for school, then go to work, come home, and look after the family while keeping a strong relationship with God - it can be a lot to handle."

Kika thought about the life Ola just described. Kika only had to wake up early for work, and there are many Saturdays she spends watching Netflix and ordering take-out. She was not sure if she was ready to give up that life.

"The point I am making Kika is that you are in this season. Treasure it while you wait because you will never get these years back once you are married." Ola stated.

"Wow, Ola, you know just what to say." Kika's spirit was lifted.

"God is good!" Ola said, "Oh, and lastly, about your job - I think it is a great blessing in disguise."

"Really, why?" Kika asked. "That was my dream job."

"No, it was not. You should never be a slave to your job. This lady had been treating you poorly for eight years. She knew you did not value yourself and you were ready to drop everything, including your self-esteem, to work for her. This is the reason she did not value you. As soon as you showed her, you could stand up for yourself, she could not handle the grace in your life."

Kika thought genuinely about what Ola said, "but where do I go from here?"

"I think you need to pray and fast about why God needed you out of that job - because Kika, there is a reason for everything, and it is going to work out altogether for your good. Trust me."

Kika smiled. Ola was speaking volumes tonight. What was funny was that this is exactly how Kika would talk to others who were in a dark spot. It was nice getting it in return. She did not only feel super encouraged, but she also felt she could conquer the world.

"Thank you so much, Ola! I feel a lot better. I have to go now, I have a dinner date with Mimi in an hour, and I have not even started getting ready!" Kika laughed.

"Ha ha, my pleasure."

Mimi

"So, who is coming today?" Dami asked Mimi as they were heading into the restaurant for her celebration dinner.

"Well, Anita is not picking up my calls, Tara told me that she and Bode were unable to make it, so I guess it is just you, me and Kika," Mimi said in a snarky way. She could understand if Tara chose never to speak to her again but still felt Tara should be honest about her feelings. Mimi also felt that when she was pregnant with her twin boys, she did not blank her friends like Anita had done. She had not even checked on her with everything that was going on - she began to wonder whether Anita had decided that she wanted nothing more to do with her, the 'Fraudulent Mimi'.

"So tell me more about Kika and why you think we

will make a great match," Dami asked, teasing Mimi. They were both seated, waiting for Kika to arrive.

"Well, personality-wise you both are total opposites," Mimi said, laughing.

"Opposites? How so?" Dami inquired.

"Well, she's fun and jovial."

"Gee, thanks," Dami said sarcastically, "You are implying that I am dull?"

"Not at all, I just feel you will balance each other out. She can bring out the spontaneity in you, and you can bring out the earnest person in her," Mimi joked.

Dami gave her a displeasing look.

"Look, Dami, opposites attract, but you do have similarities that I believe are really important. Like you are both hardworking, strong Christians who work with young people; you have the same sense of humour and are attractive." Mimi said, giving Dami a cheeky wink.

Dami laughed, "okay, well, in that case - I can't wait!"

Mimi smiled just as her phone vibrated.

"Oh, my goodness!" She shrieked.

Dami swiftly looked over at Mimi, who was staring at her phone with her eyes widened and slowly moving her head from side to side.

"What is going on?" He asked.

"Well, I have just received two separate consultation requests for events. I now feel people do believe I had nothing to do with the whole Rayo situation." Mimi said excitedly. "I am slowly getting my clients back."

Dami clapped his hands, "Well, that is great to hear! I should also tell you, since this is your celebration dinner, that some of the victims have dropped the charges against you and are concentrating on finding the actual culprit - Rayo, instead. So, congratulations, Mimi!"

"What! Really? Thanks so much! We should pop a

bottle of champagne at this point," She said, immediately signalling to the waiter.

"Yes, we can have a meeting tomorrow to run through the details. Tonight, I want you just to have a good time." Dami said, raising his champagne glass to make a toast to Mimi. "To being free!"

"To being free!" Mimi screamed in excitement while clinking her glass with Dami's. She took a sip and picked up her phone to respond to the messages. "Any news on the location of Rayo?" She said without looking up from her phone and trying not to show any feeling of fear.

"Not yet, but I do think that now that you are getting back to business, we need to ensure you are protected wherever you go," said Dami.

Mimi agreed. She did not want to be in and out of meetings and events, trembling and wondering whether Rayo was going to pop out from behind a bush.

"So what do you suggest," she asked.

"Well, I would say put a tracker in your phone and a tracker in your car?" Dami said, "That way, we can keep a watchful eye on you wherever you go, and if something were to happen to your phone, we would still be able to locate you using your car."

Mimi smiled nervously. She could not believe that this was what her life had come to. "Yes, well, I guess that makes some sort of sense."

Dami could sense her fear "You will be fine," he assured her.

At that moment, Kika walked in, looking gorgeous as usual.

"Hey, Kika!" Mimi screamed, calling her from the entrance.

"Is she always this late?" Dami asked, knowing he was being cheeky.

Mimi playfully smacked him on his arm, "pretty much." She admitted.

"Hi guys, sorry I am late," Kika said anxiously. She ran over to Mimi to give her a hug.

"Kika, this is my lawyer, Dami," Mimi said, smiling.

Kika looked at Dami; he seemed strangely familiar.

"Hi, lovely to meet you," Dami said as he put his hand out to shake her."

"Hi, have we met?" Kika said while shaking his hands and gazing into his eyes.

Dami looked into Kika's eyes and smiled. He remembered the crazy lady that hit his car.

"I believe we have," he said, laughing.

Kika knew she could not forget a beautiful face like his. Dami was the man in the Range Rover that she had an altercation with a few weeks ago.

"Oh, wow, you guys know each other already?" Mimi asked, entirely taken by surprise at this.

"Let's just say we have 'bumped' into each other in the past," Dami joked.

"I see what you did there," Kika said, trying not to smile at his cheesy joke.

During the dinner, Mimi noticed a lot of flirting between Kika and Dami. She would say something; he would laugh. He would say something; she would brush her hand on his shoulder. Mimi felt she was third-wheeling at her own celebratory dinner.

"So, Kika, what do you do?" Dami asked.

Kika felt nervous. Does she tell him that she just lost her job and was trying to figure out her life and her next move?

"Well, I used to work for 'Hello Lagos' as a writer. I just left," Kika finally said.

"You left?" Mimi asked, "Did you leave because of me?"

"No, no, it is not your fault; it was time. It is no secret how unhappy I was there. Your situation just made it final."

"I am lost," Dami said.

"Kika had worked for 'Hello Lagos' for eight years, and her boss refused to promote her. She offered her a career-boosting promotion if she would betray me, and Kika refused. I am guessing she may have…fired you?"

"Yes, she did, and I am unsure what is next for me if I am honest," she said, putting her head down in shame. Kika was nervous that a successful man like Dami will look down on her because she was jobless. But she felt she needed to be honest either way.

"Wow, that is horrible. Good on you for standing up for what you believe in. Integrity goes a long way," Dami said finally.

"Plus, Kika started this stationery collection, which is all about encouraging women," Mimi added. "I have been telling her to write a blog and become an influencer." She turned to Kika, "You seriously have a heart of gold and have so many connections. We will all listen to what you have to say," Mimi said passionately.

"Me? An influencer. I don't know about that," Kika laughed.

"Kika, you love writing, you love taking pictures, and you are passionate about women."

"I agree with Mimi. If you do love all these things, I can see why God wanted to remove you from 'Hello Lagos'. That media company is so quick to put women down - see what they even wrote about Mimi," Dami said encouragingly.

Mimi noticed how Dami naturally connected with Kika. She felt Dami could be the one for her.

"So, you liked him?" Mimi asked, feeling like she had done a perfect job at playing Cupid.

"Liked him? I have bumped into him in the past, and he was very rude to me." Kika said as she followed Mimi into her home.

Mimi was unconvinced. The whole dinner, she had felt like a third wheel because Kika and Dami could not keep their eyes off each other. "Were we at the same dinner?" Mimi joked, "you guys were talking non-stop."

"That is because I know how to keep a conversation flowing - it is called being polite, plus talking is in my nature," Kika said while flicking her weave.

Mimi shook her head; this was typical of Kika. When it came to men, she would always self-destruct before anything had even come of it. Kika claimed that she had gone through insecurities in the past, but that she was over it and is now living a life free of them. But Mimi always felt that although Kika had indeed come out of that inse-cure place, there were times it would creep back up on her.

"So, are you saying no to him if he asks you out?" Mimi asked.

"Well, when the time comes, we shall see," Kika said, keeping her cards close to her chest. "So, did you have fun tonight?" She said, changing the subject.

"I did! It was much needed after the past few months." Mimi said a bit uneasily.

"Is there something wrong?" Kika asked, picking up on Mimi's tone.

"Well, I just feel I have lost my friends," Mimi said, tearing up.

"What do you mean, who am I to you?" Kika said, trying to make light out of the situation.

"I mean, I invited all you girls tonight. I know Tara is unhappy with me, which is why she and Bode did not come, and Anita has pretty much abandoned me." Mimi was so hurt by Anita, especially when she knows she did nothing wrong.

Kika felt guilty. Out of all the girls, only she knew about Anita's situation and all she was going through. It had nothing to do with Mimi. In fact, Anita was even flipping out on her. She pondered a way to ease Mimi's emotions without stabbing Anita in the back.

"Look, Mimi, listen to me. Tara is upset without a doubt, but trust me when I tell you it's got nothing to do with you. Please understand that Tara has just lost N2 billion. This money was going to go into her 'over the top' wedding and help launch her business. Her and Bode have a lot on their plate at the moment, as do you. Don't take their quietness personally. Once we catch Rayo and everyone hopefully gets their money back, this will all be sorted, okay?" Kika expressed from the heart.

Mimi sniffled, "Okay, I guess so. Thank you, Kika."

Kika was nicely surprised that she managed to get through her little speech without bringing up Anita.

"But what about Anita?" Mimi asked.

"Spoke too soon," Kika said under her breath and sighed. "Okay, Mimi, something massive is happening in Anita's life, and she made me promise not to tell anyone. I can tell you that she is also going through a rough time. Life is just not being fair and is attacking everyone in different ways right now. We just have to pray that God gets us all through this difficult time." Kika said, impressed again that she said enough to comfort Mimi, but not too much to betray her loyalty to Anita.

Just like that, Mimi realised that she had been so focused on herself and had not thought about what others may be going through.

Although she did not know precisely what Anita was dealing with, she knew it must be really hurtful for her not to respond to any messages or check up on her. She also realised that she was probably paranoid about Tara. She knew the whole situation hurt her friend, and here she was, more bothered about whether her friend would forgive her or not.

"I have been so conceited," Mimi blurted out.

Kika laughed. "No, you do have your own problems."

At that point, Mimi's phone began to ring.

"Oh wow, it's Tara," Mimi said to Kika in shock.

"You see! Pick it up," Kika screamed.

"Hey, Tara," Mimi said.

"Mimi darling, I am so sorry once again that Bode and I were unable to make it tonight," Tara said, sounding genuinely remorseful.

"Oh it's fine, I know you have a lot going on at the moment."

"Yes, I do, which is part of the reason I am calling. I know it's late, but I am launching my fashion collection and want to do a photoshoot tomorrow. Kika and my cousin Dabira will be modelling. I was wondering if you can be one of the models, too, please?" Tara asked.

Mimi was over the moon - she knew that this was the confirmation she needed to be sure that Tara was indeed not holding her responsible for their loss, the fact that she still wanted her to be a part of her business. She was very excited.

"Of course, I will."

A journal to the reader

Dear Reader,

My heart bleeds for Kika in this chapter. She has the desire to meet the right person, and there is no particular reason why she hasn't. She is not doing anything wrong. Ola said it perfectly. It all comes down to God's perfect timing.

Ecclesiastes 3:1 says, "There is a time for everything and a season for every activity under the heavens..."

God has planned everything concerning you and will make it all work together for good. (Romans 8:28)

I have learned from waiting for marriage myself that God understands that it is not easy, that he said he would renew our strength while we wait. (Isaiah 40:31)

From a young age, I always envisioned myself getting married at 24 like Kika, because my mum and a lot of my female family members got married at that age. To me, it seemed automatic that once I finish university, marriage was my next step.

That was not the plan God had for me. If it were, it would have happened by now. He has needed me to grow, work on myself, and accomplish things that maybe I needed to achieve before marriage.

I mean for one, I would not be writing this journal now if I were married, I'd appeal to a different demographic, and God clearly wanted me to appeal to singles.

How I overcame the obsession was realising that it is important to be content in whatever season you find yourself in; and to do it well, meaning you live that season to the fullest.

If you are single, do it well. If you are married, do it well. If you are studying, do it well. If you are a mother, do it well.

Habakkuk 2:3: "For still the vision awaits its appointed time; it hastens to the end - it will not lie. If it seems slow, wait for it; it will surely come; it will not delay."

At God's appointed time, whatever you are waiting for will happen - it will not delay. It could be the perfect job, waiting for a child, buying your first home. It could be anything.

As you wait, ensure that you do not compare yourself to others. Comparison is a thief of joy.

Also, the fact that someone has achieved these things you desire does not make them any more special or valuable than you are. It was just what God had planned for them, and if you think about your life, I am sure you can see multiple ways God has blessed you, ahead of others.

Journal Task 11: Write down a list of things that God has done for you in your life on one side of the page. Now write a list on the other side of what you are believing God for. Then say this prayer:

Dear God, you know the desires of my heart. You know the end from my beginning. I ask that you please renew my strength as I wait; and give me the grace to live this season I am in to the fullest. In Jesus' name. Amen!

Tip: Love your journey; it is specific to you - Y.S.P

Lots of Love X

Simi Alexis Romeo

CHAPTER TWELVE

Kika

[Hi Kika, this is Dami. It was so great seeing you tonight. I hope you don't mind. I asked Mimi for your number. How are you?]

Kika was excited about Mr Dami Dare. He seemed like a good guy. He had really been there and supportive of Mimi, more than could reasonably be expected from him just being her lawyer, which just showed his heart. He feared God, which was very hard to find in this day and age, especially in Lagos.

"I wonder why he is single?" she said to herself. She was sceptical because he seemed perfect. She rang him back.

"Hey, I was not expecting you to call," Dami said, laughing.

"I just feel you get to know someone a lot more when you talk," Kika responded.

"That makes sense," Dami said, still trying to stop

himself from laughing. "So should we start from the beginning - you know you hit my car," he said, thinking that making light of the incident would break the ice.

"I am not going to keep going over this, Dami. You are just lucky that you did not scratch my car, because I would have billed you big time, now I know that you are Mimi's lawyer." She said, laughing. "Speaking of Mimi, I am guessing she is safe from Rayo now?"

"Well, not exactly, her doing the interview was a way to lure Rayo into coming back to town. We need to bring him back to Lagos from wherever he went so he can be arrested."

"But doesn't that put Mimi at great risk? He is crazy, what if he like, kills her?" Kika said nervously.

"It is tricky, but we have tried hard to put some protective measures in place to ensure Mimi's safety. For example, we have put a tracker on her phone and her car. I shouldn't be telling you this, but I feel I can trust you. I know you have the best intentions for her."

Kika smiled, already Dami trusts her. She could not stop blushing. She was so happy the conversation was over the phone, so Dami could not see her grinning from ear to ear like a 'loser'.

"All we can do now is pray," Dami continued.

Kika thought about what Dami said. She understood that a tracker was put in her phone and car, but those things can so quickly be taken away from her if an abduction were to occur. In her heart, she did not feel okay about it, but she was not going to dampen the mood by talking about the situation.

"So Mr Dare, why are you single - what is wrong with you?" She asked cheekily.

Dami laughed, "I could say the same about you, Miss Taiwo."

Kika laughed.

"I don't know; I guess I just have not found the right person. My last relationship was about four years ago. She cheated on me with my then best friend. It was the worst thing possible because I was about to propose to her. And worse, my friend knew that."

Kika was in shock, "Oh my goodness, that is horrible!"

"Yes it is, they even got married to each other. I was so deeply hurt by it that I now have a great issue with trusting people. I just put all my energy into my work, and it has paid off," Dami said.

"Would you say you have healed from the pain you went through?" Kika asked.

"Well, I don't know. I am certainly hoping to heal from it. In trying to do so, I had to forgive both my ex and my ex-friend - that took a while. I realised that they are happy, living their best lives, having kids, and I am alone unhappy. I am such a hopeless romantic, so I wanted love. But by getting closer to God, I realised that the fact they are together was God's plan all along for them and me. They found their soulmates in each other - unfortunately, it was at my expense. But God needed to toughen me up for a higher purpose, I guess."

"Would you say you are stronger?" Kika asked.

"Absolutely, when I look back, I don't think we would have been happy either. She wanted to be a housewife and not work at a career or business - whereas I appreciate a woman who does. It would have caused us problems," Dami continued.

"Wow, thanks for being open and honest with me," Kika said, still mesmerised by Dami's story. She would never be able to forgive a friend if they betrayed her like that.

"I have to be. I have not had a connection like this for

years. I want to be open and honest with you, just as much as I hope you will be open and honest with me?" Dami continued. Kika was in awe. "So tell me about this blog that Mimi was talking about."

"Well, there is no blog," Kika clarified, "I have started a stationery collection to encourage people. It includes journals with words of affirmations and cards with scriptures on it."

"That is an amazing idea - does it work?" Dami asked enthusiastically.

"Well, every one of my friends is going through some struggle or the other right now, and I gave them all the cards to encourage them, and the feedback has been amazing. One of them gave her life to Christ just from reading them," Kika said, thinking about Anita. "I actually went through a tough time a few years back with loving myself and appreciating my life. These words helped me overcome them - this is the reason why I wanted to have a segment at 'Hello Lagos' where I could empower women."

"That is awesome, Kika! You know this woman empowerment stuff seems to be your calling. If you love to write, why don't you just write? The purpose is to help people, so that should be your focus," Dami encouraged. "Oh, and might I just add, I believe God needed you out of 'Hello Lagos'. Sometimes a dead-end is a dead-end because God has something better in store for you."

"Yeah, I guess you are right," she said, blushing.

"Honestly, start that blog. I think Mimi is right."

Kika was at a loss for words. She was quite surprised by how supportive Dami was, especially as he hardly knew her.

"Well, it is getting late, but before we head to bed, I would love to take you out sometime," Dami said nervously, "So would you go on a date with me?" He asked.

Kika giggled, "I'd love to, good night, Dami Dare."

"Goodnight, Kika."

Kika woke up early to get ready for Tara's photoshoot. All night, all she could think about was Dami. She had never felt so comfortable with any guy like the way she felt with him. He seemed so genuine - and she just had a sense of peace about him.

She quickly got her journal from her bedside table.

[Dear God, I met Dami last night. He seems so genuine. Is he the one?]

She closed her journal and hoped that God would give her a clear sign about him.

She put on some loungewear and quickly headed to her car. Unusually, she was early because she wanted to make a quick stop to get a present for Mimi. She attended her celebratory dinner and had not bought her anything.

"That's not very kind," she joked to herself.

Tara

"Okay, Dabira, you look great, turn towards the left! Beautiful! That's great!" The photographer was calling out on the set.

Mimi and Tara were sat watching the girls model Tara's first collection.

"Tara, this looks amazing, it looks so professional. Thank you for not boycotting me and still letting me be a part of your life," Mimi said with gratitude.

"Mimi, I have known you for years. You are a good person. What Rayo has done is disgusting, and I know you have never been, are not, nor will ever be a part of such," Tara comforted.

"Thanks, Tara!"

"So, Bode and I were thinking of holding an intimate games night with our close friends and family, like a pre-wedding get-together next Friday evening?" Tara said.

"Instead of something or in addition to?" Mimi asked.

"Well, instead of all the pointless pre-wedding activities I wanted to have," Tara laughed.

Mimi was surprised by Tara's awakening. She knew Tara was cutting back due to the effects of Rayo's antics, but she seemed okay about it.

"Anyway, I would love you to come," Tara said, smiling.

Mimi smiled "I am sure it will be the best games night ever, but I can't. I am on a curfew to keep me safe from Rayo. I have already promised my lawyer I would restrict going out in the evenings as much as possible. Plus, I am so busy with the kids next Friday."

"Yeah, that makes sense. Maybe we can 'Zoom' you in." Tara understood that Mimi was also going through a rough time. "So how is everything going anyways with Rayo, you and the kids?" Tara continued.

"Well the police are still trying to find him, I mean, how far could he have gone?" Mimi said, distressed. "The kids are good, they are little troopers, and I try to distract them as much as possible. Me? Well, I have lost a lot of business as you can imagine, but it's slowly picking up again, so I am just trying to get through."

"Yeah, well, aren't we all."

Mimi gave Tara a weird look, and Tara quickly realised how that had come across and apologised.

"It is fine, Tara. I am again really sorry about everything."

"No, it is fine, sorry it just came out!"

"So where's Kika?" Mimi quickly said, changing the subject.

"Well, she said she had to pick up something, but she should be on her way now," Tara said, looking at her watch.

"Okay, Dabira, perfect! You can go for a break now. Mimi, it is your turn to take some shots." the photographer yelled.

As Mimi made her way to the set, Dabira rushed into the bathroom.

Tara could not help but notice how sick Dabira looked and quickly followed her, a tad concerned.

When she got to the bathroom, she found Dabira on her knees, heaving into the toilet.

"Oh my goodness, Dabira, are you okay?" Tara ran to her side. She held back Dabira's hair but couldn't help but worry about the prototype from her fashion line that Dabira was wearing.

"Yes, yes, I am so, so sorry," Dabira pleaded.

"Dabira, what is going on? Are you okay?" Tara asked, worried.

"Tara, I am pregnant!"

"What?!" Since Dabira arrived, Tara had noticed several signs that made her wonder if she could be pregnant, but not for a second did she feel that it could actually be true.

"Since when?"

"Erm, like four months - which is why it is so bizarre that I am still dealing with morning sickness," Dabira said, getting up and sitting on the toilet lid.

"Four months and you hid it from me this whole time?" Tara said, annoyed.

"Yes, well, I knew you'd ask me about my boyfriend in London." Dabira continued.

"You have a boyfriend in London?"

"Not exactly, I don't."

"You have a boyfriend in Lagos?" Tara asked, raising her eyebrows.

At this point, Dabira had become stressed out. "No!"

"Calm down Dabira, was it a one night stand?" Tara asked carefully.

"Tara, promise me that you won't tell anyone what I am about to tell you!"

"I promise, and I swear on my life," Tara began to feel anxious.

"Well, the truth is, I am pregnant for a married man in Lagos. I cannot tell you who it is, so please do not ask." Dabira said quickly.

Tara was in complete shock. She stared at Dabira in disbelief, her mouth open.

"I am sorry, but he wants nothing to do with me or the baby and begged me to abort the child. But I could never do such a thing. I am so against abortion, imagine if your mother got what she wanted, I would have never had a cousin turned sister in my life, and you have had such a positive impact on my life."

"Well, clearly not that positive if you are getting pregnant for married men," Tara said under her breath.

"We have been having an affair for years. At first, I did not know he was married. I found out on the blog - 'Hello Lagos' - as he is quite a popular guy. But at that point, I was in too deep, and he told me he was going to leave her for me. A few months ago, he came to London for a conference and, well yeah, now I'm pregnant," she said under her breath as she rubbed her belly. "I came to Lagos to try and sort it out with him, but he has treated me so poorly." Dabira began to cry.

Tara did not really know what to say. She could not believe her own flesh and blood was the type of girl who would do this. But she knew Dabira's heart. Dabira was a kind soul who wanted the best for everyone. She made a mistake, and now she has to deal with the consequences.

"Look, Dabira, this is not an ideal situation. It is messed up, but you are my sister, and I love you. I will be there for you through thick and thin. You are not alone - this is our baby." Tara said while hugging her.

Dabira began to weep and returned the hug, "I love you, Tara."

Kika

Kika could not believe the conversation she had just heard from outside the bathroom. She had not meant to invade on Tara and Dabira's private conversation. She had come in late to the photoshoot and wanted to freshen up in the bathroom. However, she was in shock at hearing Dabira's story, and as the dots slowly started to connect in her mind.

Dabira is pregnant for a popular married man. Dabira lives in London, and Dabira's name starts with a 'D', Kika thought to herself. Could Nati's mistress be Dabira? Kika could not be sure, but she knew what her gut was telling her. The fact that Dabira refuses to tell Tara who the person is was probably because she knew Tara and Anita were best of friends.

Kika turned around from the bathroom - she felt sick. Although Anita had told her that D had agreed to have an abortion, she did not trust Nati enough to believe him, and it didn't seem so from the conversation she had just overheard.

"Are you okay, Kika?" Mimi asked when she walked back on set.

"I don't feel very well. I have to go. Please send my apologies to Tara," Kika said without any emotion in her face. "Here, I got you a present for the celebratory dinner - sorry it is late."

"Aww, you shouldn't have. Are you okay, though?" Mimi said while opening the gift, "Aww, these diamond earrings are gorgeous. Thank you, Kika." She said, hugging her.

"Yes, well, they are studs that you can wear every day so that you can look great for this new chapter in your life - every day," Kika smiled.

Mimi laughed, "Well, I will wear them now," she said. "Thanks again."

"No worries, I have to go now," She hugged Mimi and ran out of the studio. She needed to get to the bottom of the mystery of Dabira's pregnancy. Although Anita and Kika had not spoken, she was still her best friend, and she owed her the truth. Kika also knew how trusting Anita was, so she knew she needed to go to her with fact and not speculation.

Anita

A few days had passed, and Anita and Kika had still not spoken. Although Anita missed her best friend, she did not feel she needed someone in her life who seemed so unwilling to support her decisions. Everything with Nati and her had become so much better, and the love between them had grown immensely.

Her phone rang.

"Hey doll, long time," Tara said enthusiastically.

Anita had not spoken to Tara in months. Although they were not as close as she and Kika were, Tara was still a very good friend. Tara was unaware of all that Anita was going through, and as far as she was concerned, Tara was planning her huge wedding, and Anita did not want to bring her down with any negative baggage.

"I am inviting you to me and Bode's pre-marital games night this Friday," Tara said excitedly. "It is a good chance to catch up with you as I have not spoken to you in months. It is very intimate - it's just a few of my best friends, their husbands, and our family. So, can you make it?"

Anita laughed, "of course I can, and I will be dragging Nati along with me." She was surprised that Tara decided to do something intimate.

"That's great! Also, one of my cousins is pregnant, so I am sure you two will have a lot to talk about," Tara said.

Anita did not want to make the conversation uncomfortable by telling Tara that she had lost the baby. She was, however, excited to meet Tara's family. They are all based in London, which was where Tara grew up and lived before she moved back to Nigeria and met Bode.

"I will see you on Friday. Bye, dear."

Later that morning, Nati and Anita were having pancakes for breakfast in the dining room.

"I have a business meeting this afternoon. My client is bringing his wife. Would you like to come?" Nati asked Anita as he reached for another pancake.

"Well," Anita sat up "I had planned to go to this orphanage I have been visiting these past few months. You should come with me actually; the children are so adorable, Nati," she exclaimed.

Nati raised his eyebrows at Anita.

"Are you trying to manipulate me into adoption, Anita? I told you how I feel about that. Plus, I do not think now is a good time for a baby," Nati said sternly.

"No, I don't want to adopt," Anita reassured him. She sat back in her seat. She had forgotten how controlling Nati could be. It was either his way or the highway. Anita had meekly fallen in line before the cheating, but something has changed within her since then.

"But Nati, I really would like to go to the orphanage today," she pleaded.

"I love that you care so much about these children, it is very admirable. However, you have made a commitment to be in this relationship, and therefore you should not neglect your duties as the woman of this home," he said strictly. "The meeting is at 2 pm. I will send the car to pick you at 1:30."

Before Anita could respond, he had gotten up, kissed her on the forehead, and walked into the bedroom, without a second glance.

She felt herself back in a place where she could not stand up for herself. She was fed up with going to these pretentious meetings where she had to show off to Nati's clients that they were this perfect couple, and he was the most trustworthy and ideal husband and businessman, which was usually the case; this time however, she had to pretend.

She felt incredibly guilty that she was not going to be able to see Caleb. She had developed such a deep connection with all of the children at the orphanage, but Nati was right; she had had the time to be there for Caleb because marital duties were suspended while she was staying with

Kika. But as she had now made the decision to return and be with Nati, she could no longer turn her back on her conjugal obligations. Although she felt torn, she knew she had to support Nati and accompany him to the meeting.

"My decision determines my destiny," she said to herself, remembering Kika's wise words.

A journal to the reader

Dear Reader,

Over the last few chapters, Mimi had felt very uncomfortable around not just her close friends, but with society in general. Rayo had painted her to be someone that she was not, by stealing from her clients and friends, and she ended up feeling isolated. What was worse was that she had not heard much from Anita and Tara, two of her best friends.

Sometimes in life, God needs to isolate you for a greater purpose. He needs you to have nothing else or no one else to rely on except Him. God is kind, so he will not give you more than you can handle, and will surround you with people that will comfort you in the way you need to be. With Mimi, God surrounded her with the love of her mother, the love of her friend Kika and her lawyer, Dami Dare.

All the characters have been going through some life-changing issues, and at a point, they each felt isolated and alone.

Anita felt isolated when she lost Nati and her baby, but God still gave her the comfort of Kika, who helped her believe in God and develop her faith.

Tara felt isolated when her dreams were shattered by her and Bode losing all their money, but God gave her Pastor Lade.

Kika had already established a relationship with God. However, she needed to delve deeper into that relationship, and God still gave her Ola from her mid-week fellowship to rely on.

I think these all show God's love and kindness.

In a previous journal, I mentioned how I had been going through a tough time during the 2020 Pandemic self-isolation period. Naturally, I am a homebody, and I do love spending time by myself. However, I did not think then that I would be tackling them alone when I was going through all these things. During that period, I was desperate for a hug and some comfort. God was still so kind; he gave me listening ears. Many of my family and friends kept checking on me to make sure I was okay and provided me with love and comfort. However, when I wake up at 2 am panicking and worried, who else can I rely on other than God. He was my comforter and my best friend during that time - He still is. He encouraged me a lot, and my relationship grew stronger. I was able to be sensitive to the spirit, and in fact, I was able to write this book during that period as well. Sometimes God births things out of you during your most trying times.

If you feel isolated, try your best to remember who God is. He does not want you to be upset; he wants to build you up and grow you. He wants to give you hope and a future. (Jeremiah 29:11)

Journal Task 12: Write a list of who you think God is to you. And whenever you are in a period of isolation, go back to this list and remember he is here to comfort you.

Tip: Use the scriptures below to help you with the journal task. There are so many more verses and stories in the Bible that show who God is:

Genesis 1:1 - He is the creator
1 Corinthians 10:13 - He is faithful
2 Peter:3:9 - He is patient
Numbers 23:19 - He does not lie
Psalm 116:5 - He is compassionate
Micah 7 18-19 - He is merciful

Lots of Love X

Simi Alexis Romeo

CHAPTER THIRTEEN

Anita

"Nati, I am nervous about seeing Kika tonight," Anita said while putting on her mascara.

They were getting ready for Tara's pre-marital games night, and Anita knew she owed Kika an apology. Bringing up her single life, which she knows is one of Kika's greatest insecurities, was taking it too far.

"You guys have been friends for years, I am sure you will sort it out tonight," Nati comforted.

Anita swiftly picked up her handbag, walked out of the house, and got into the car's passenger seat. Nati followed her out while putting on his blazer. He locked the front door and headed to the driver's side.

"So, is it just me that feels it is weird that Tara is having such an intimate event. She usually prefers these over the top parties?" Anita questioned, still unaware of the events relating to Rayo defrauding Bode.

Nati gave Anita a confused look, "Well yeah, they have to cut back after all they have been through?"

"What have they been through?" Anita asked.

Nati realised that Anita had probably not been in touch with her friends or happenings in the world, ever since the crisis and her move-in with Kika. "Remember that massive deal Rayo wanted us to invest in, and before I did, you sent me a text not to go for it?"

"Yeah?" she said.

"Well, it was a fake deal. Rayo ended up absconding with N5 billion of people's money that day, and now, no one can find him. Mimi has had to deal with the backlash."

"What!?"

"Yes. Bode actually put up N2 billion of the N5 billion that was stolen, which was most of all they owned. Honestly, thank God you had that premonition, and you sent me that text. We may have been in a very different place financially right now."

"Oh, my goodness, are you serious?" Anita was flabbergasted.

She had been so focused on her loss; she was unaware that her friends were going through their own struggles. Mimi had been reaching out, but she ignored her because she did not want to have to discuss her own issues with her. She had tried Tara a few times because she knew Tara would probably just talk about the wedding, and hopefully distract her from her loss. Tara, however, had not been picking up her calls.

"I cannot believe this, wow!" Anita said, staring into the distance, still in shock.

Nati looked over at Anita and laughed, "wow, have you been living under a rock? It has literally been all over the streets of Lagos."

Anita rolled her eyes. If Nati was focused on his marriage and not the streets, she probably would have been able to be there for her friends more. All of a sudden, a text message came through from Kika.

[Hey hun, I know we haven't spoken, but I really need to talk to you tonight. Love and miss you X]

"Oh, my goodness, Kika just sent me a message - she wants to talk tonight, too," Anita said, excited.

"Oh great, that's perfect babe, I told you, you guys will work it through," Nati assured her.

She looked out of the window and made a sigh of relief. She was glad that she and Kika were back in a good place. She felt guilty that she had not been there for her friends, but hopefully, when they see her belly, they would understand why she had been out of the loop. "Thank you, God!" She whispered under her breath, smiling to herself.

Nati and Anita arrived at Tara's home in Lekki. They couldn't wait to let their hair down and have a night of fun, given how dramatic the past few months had been. She knocked on the door, and Bode answered it.

"If it isn't my favourite couple," he said, shaking Nati's hand and hugging Anita.

Tara shrieked with excitement and began to run towards Anita. As she approached her and saw the size of her stomach, she slowed down, and an extremely concerned look was suddenly plastered across her face.

"Surprise, surprise! Unfortunately, I lost the baby, and I had no idea how to tell you," Anita said sarcastically.

"Oh no, Anita, you one hundred percent should have told me," she said in dismay while wrapping Anita in her arms. "I hope you are okay! I am so sorry I did not pick up your calls. I have been going through stuff myself." Tara said, feeling guilty.

"I only just heard. I am so sorry about everything,"

Anita began to tear up. "Is Mimi here, I need to apologise for not being there for her too."

"Her lawyer has put her on a curfew, so she could not make it. How are you though, tell me?" Tara asked.

"I am fine; it has been a few months now. I still most definitely want to meet your cousin though, and where's Kika?"

This was typical of Anita. She never blamed others for her misfortune. She always wanted to celebrate others, and this was why she hadn't stopped feeling guilty about not doing anything to stop D having an abortion.

"Kika has nipped to the supermarket to get some snacks. She will be here soon, but in the meantime, let me introduce you to my cousin, Dabira," Tara said while gradually pulling out her right arm to direct Anita and Nati's attention to this gorgeous pregnant woman.

Anita looked up at Nati and smiled, but Nati's face was a picture. His eyes had widened, and he looked incredibly shell-shocked.

"This is my gorgeous cousin, Dabira! She's expecting!" Tara said, extremely excited to introduce her cousin to one of her oldest friends.

Anita turned around to see this beautiful woman standing in front of her. She was tall and dark in complexion. She had long, jet black hair with her edges laid to perfection. She had big, gorgeous eyes that were accompanied with cat-eyed eyelashes. Her skin was flawless, smile was perfect, and she had a beautiful, little baby bump.

Dabira looked at both Anita and Nati; her face froze. She had had no idea they would be coming, especially as Tara hadn't been in touch with them since she arrived in Lagos.

Confused, Anita continued to introduce herself. "Hi, I'm Anita, and this is my husband, Nati."

Anita put her hand out to shake Dabira.

Dabira smiled awkwardly and reciprocated the handshake.

"Hi, I am Dabira. Lovely to meet you both."

"Erm… I need to get a drink, do you want something hun?" Nati nervously asked Anita.

"A glass of red wine would be nice, hunny," she smiled. She could not understand why she could feel this awkward tension, and why Nati was acting weird.

Nati went over quickly to the house bar to make himself a drink, but more like to avoid the situation at hand and give himself some time to think.

At that moment, Kika walked into the living room with some snacks and saw Dabira and Anita standing with each other talking. She had detailed information and was ready to disclose everything.

"Hey, Ani, can we please talk," Kika knew she was somewhat rude by interrupting their conversation. Still, she knew that once Anita found out who Dabira was, they would not be having any communication whatsoever.

"Hey, Kika," Anita smiled. She was keen to resolve any issues they had, "Sure!" She excused herself from Dabira and followed Kika into Bode's study.

"Kika, I am so sorry about how I spoke to you last time we saw each other. After everything you have done for me. I should know you were just trying to help," Anita said, shamefaced.

"Ani, I forgave you a long time ago, and I am sorry about how I spoke to you too. Honestly, we have bigger fish to fry. There is something I need to tell you." Kika gave Anita a concerned look.

"What's the problem?" Anita's heart began to beat fast.

Kika sighed, "Dabira is D."

"What do you mean?"

"Like D, Nati's mistress, stands for Dabira, Tara's cousin." Kika continued.

"I am not understanding, are you saying Dabira is Nati's mistress?" Anita questioned.

Kika nodded.

"That makes no sense because Dabira is pregnant, and Nati told me D got rid of the baby."

"She did not, Anita! I overheard Tara and Dabira talking during Tara's photoshoot event. Dabira mentioned how she had an affair with a married man and got pregnant." Kika explained, "She said, the married man told her he wants nothing to do with her, but she refused to tell Tara who it was, and I think it is because she knows you are Nati's wife, and she is aware how close you and Tara are." She paused to gauge Anita's reaction.

"So, you are speculating that it's Nati, you don't actually know?" Anita said defensively.

"Well, I do. I did some more digging and found out that Dabira and Nati have mutual friends in London, and there is one I am actually quite close to. She told me that they were together at a boat party and could not keep their hands off each other. Apparently, they left the party holding hands." Kika would never want to bring such sensitive news without being a hundred percent sure it happened - it was the journalist inside of her.

Anita's jaw began to clench. She did not feel upset; she was done crying over Nati. This time, she was angry and knew she needed to get all the details from Dabira as she could not trust a word that came out of Nati's mouth.

"Are you okay?" Kika asked anxiously.

"I need to speak to her!" Anita charged out of the study and made her way back to the living room with Kika following close behind.

Nati saw Anita approaching Dabira and Tara, and

quickly tried to remove himself from the situation by going to the bathroom. But before he could make it to the door, he found Kika standing in his way.

"Really, Nati? You cannot even take responsibility for your actions," She said with a sense of disappointment.

He knew Kika was right. He knew that once again, he had made a mess of everything. He remorsefully headed back to where all the ladies were standing - but allowing a good enough distance from them.

Dabira smiled as Anita approached her, unaware she had just found out.

"So, my husband, Nati," Anita looked at Nati as he stood by, sweating and feeling uncomfortable, "is that his baby in there?"

Tara spat out her drink, "What?! Is this the married man you fell pregnant for Dabira - my best friend's husband?"

"I thought you got rid of the baby?" Anita questioned.

Dabira started shaking.

'Well, answer her," Tara yelled.

"I am so sorry, Anita. Initially, I had no idea that Nati was married. When I found out, I was already in too deep. If I had known you were Tara's friend prior, I never would have gone there," Dabira said, feeling guilty.

"Should you be going for married men at all?" Anita was furious. Why was Dabira trying to justify her actions?

Dabira sighed. "Nati has told me that he wants nothing to do with me or the baby. He said if I decide to go through with the pregnancy, he or she will grow up without a father," Dabira continued.

Anita looked at Nati - he was looking down. He knew he had indeed broken the trust in their relationship again. He had lied to Anita that Dabira had willingly gotten rid of the baby. She thought back to the time she felt God had told her to give Dabira a call, and she ignored the pushing. If she had called, she would have known Nati was lying to her.

"Nati, what on earth have you turned into?" Anita expressed furiously, "you want to kill a baby you willingly helped make, and if Dabira refuses to abort the pregnancy, you were prepared to disown your own child - especially knowing how much of a struggle it has been for me to get pregnant." She began to throw her hands at him, "and knowing you have already unintentionally killed my baby - who the hell do you think you are?"

"I didn't mean to lie to you; I just didn't want a reminder of the mistake I made and how much I hurt you. I thought you would be relieved if you thought the baby was gone, and we could just go back to the way we were."

"Of course, it is not what I want, Nati. I want to find a way to move forward with our relationship. My own concern was whether or not I could live with the fact that you have another baby. I never wanted to kill a child."

Nati looked around the room. The whole party was staring at them; he put his head down in abject humiliation.

"How are we supposed to move forward with a child though, Anita. We would have to keep Dabira in our lives," he said rudely, pointing at Dabira's stomach.

"Well, you made your bed Nati, go and lie in it." She slapped him, turned, and stormed out of Tara's house. Kika followed closely behind.

"Wait, Ani - wait!" Kika called to her.

Anita stopped at the car. In seconds, she realised that she had nowhere to go, no home to go to, no car to get in. She fell to her knees, weeping.

Kika caught up to her, sat on the ground, and hugged her tightly. "You don't deserve this. You are fearfully and wonderfully made, a royal diadem Anita. Know I am here for you. I love you immensely. and we are going to get through this."

Tara

Tara could not believe what had just happened at her game's night. First, she had no idea that Anita had even lost a child or had these issues with Nati. She thought back to the many times Anita had called her, and how she self-lessly thought she was calling to gloat about the fact she and Bode had lost a lot of money.

"Why would I even think Anita would ever do that?" She regretfully thought to herself.

She also could not believe that Dabira's mystery married man was Nati, Anita's perfect husband. She was torn; she wanted to be there for her best friend, but Dabira is family.

"Tara, I don't know what to say," Dabira said anxiously.

Tara raised her hand to Dabira's face. "Dabira, I really do not know how you got yourself in this mess, but you owe Anita a massive apology," she sighed, "and so do I."

She looked at Bode, who was comforting Nati while simultaneously escorting all the guests out of their house. Bode hated being a part of any drama, and getting everyone out was his priority.

Tara feared for her and Anita's friendship. Dabira was about to give birth to her best friend's husband's baby, which was most definitely going to be awkward. She went up to her bedroom to think about everything. She needed guidance - guidance from God.

Mimi

"So how is business, dear?" Mrs Coker said while changing Daniel's nappy.

"Business has really stepped up, mum. It is bizarre. At first, nobody wanted anything to do with me, but now my diary could not be busier," Mimi said happily.

Her boys were happy and healthy and reaching their milestones, her business had seen a revival and was doing exceptionally well, her relationship with her friends was better than ever, and most importantly, she was learning to rely on God more and more.

"Oh mummy, look at the gorgeous earrings Kika gave me," she said, stroking the diamond earrings and flaunting them to her mum.

"They are beautiful," Mrs Coker said stroking Mimi's earlobe. "Mimi, I am so proud of how you handled yourself during this whole episode, and I believe the Lord too is proud of you - you have let God take the wheel in your life." Mrs Coker said as she lifted Daniel into the crib and picked Desmond up to change him.

"Mum, I could not do this without you. You have really been there for me. I have learnt my strength from you," Mimi said, holding her mother tightly.

She truly believed that. If her mother had not gotten involved, who would she have been able to rely on like this? "Thanks for changing the boys, you know I hate that part," she laughed as she looked at her phone. Mimi suddenly stopped when she saw a consultation request come through.

"Oh my goodness, mummy," she exclaimed.

Mrs Coker looked up at her daughter.

"I just received an invite to consult for the governor of

Lagos's 60th birthday party. His assistant has just emailed me to meet him tonight at 9 pm." Mimi said excitedly.

"Tonight?" Mrs Coker asked. "Demilade, 9 pm is way too late, and you know you are on a curfew."

"Mum, I have had 9 pm appointments in the past," Mimi explained.

"That was before this Rayo episode and the death threats. I don't think this is safe. If someone wants to meet you, then meet them in the daytime."

Mimi paused. She understood where her mother was coming from. She was also petrified about potentially walking into a trap - but she thought about how much money she had lost over the past few months.

"Mummy, this is a great opportunity," she exclaimed. "This will put my business back on the map, especially if the governor of Lagos state is trusting me to plan his 60th birthday?"

Mrs Coker was not convinced - but there was no dissuading her daughter. When Mimi put her mind to something, she went for it.

"Maybe we should call Dami and get his thoughts?" Mrs Coker suggested.

"Good idea, mummy!" Mimi got hold of her phone to call Dami.

"Dami, I just received an invite for a meeting today at 9 pm regarding the governor's 60th birthday party, Although, I am aware 9 pm is quite late and could be unsafe, I feel this opportunity is too good to be missed." Mimi shared on the phone.

"Hmm," Dami thought to himself, "I agree, this opportunity would be too good to be missed," Dami said, still in his thoughts.

"No Dami, It is weird and unsafe, and I don't like the

idea of this. You are the one that told her she needs to be on a curfew," Mrs Coker interjected.

"Mrs Coker, Mimi is trying to get her business back. So, if she breaks the rules for one night, I think it would be fine."

"Dami, 9 pm o!" She yelled.

"Many people have business meetings at this time, especially governors who are so busy during the day. This is Lagos; it is very normal. I wish the meeting request came in advance; we would have been able to organise security for you. Just take extra caution, Mimi; we have a tracker we placed in your phone and your car, so if anything happens, we can find you immediately," Dami reassured them.

Mrs Coker was still not convinced. She sat in her room and began to pray that all will be well as Mimi went to get ready.

Kika

Kika's mind was all over the place following the revelation of the Dabira and Nati affair.

She had brought Anita back to her flat to be consoled. Kika did have prior plans for a date with Dami that evening, but once she knew all was going to come to light about Dabira, she knew Anita was going to need her and had had to reschedule.

Kika had tucked Anita into bed when she went back to her room to journal. She had felt that it was probably time for her to start the blog her friends had been bugging her to do, especially now that she was unemployed. Kika felt it was important to share her story of struggling with insecurity and getting to the point of valuing herself. She was working on the concept when a call came through from Dami.

"Hi Kika, it is a shame we did not get to hang out tonight, how is your friend?" He asked.

"She is great; she is asleep in the guest room. I can only assume she will be staying with me for a while. How are you?" asked Kika.

"I am good; I just received this frantic call from Mrs Coker, Mimi's mum," he said unbothered.

"Oh my goodness, is everything okay with Mimi?" Kika asked, worried.

"Yes, she is fine. Mrs Coker is just being a mum, worrying. Mimi has a meeting this evening with the governor of Lagos state. He wants her to plan his 60th birthday. The meeting is tonight, so she was just worried."

Kika went quiet. She could swear that the Lagos state governor already celebrated his 60th birthday a few months back. In fact, she remembered that 'Hello Lagos' covered the event.

"Hello, Kika, are you there?" Dami asked.

"Erm Dami, I think we have a problem," Kika eventually said.

Mimi

Mimi arrived at the Fountain Hotel, a boutique hotel, where she would be meeting the governor and his assistant. She was excited as this was going to be one of the most significant events she had done in a long while. She made sure she had her phone on her, in case something did happen to her - "you could never be too careful." She thought.

As she got out of her car and looked at the building, she began to wonder why a governor would come to a place like this. It seemed worn down, the paint had been scraped off the wall, and there was not much light coming from the building. Mimi began to feel extremely uncomfortable and held her phone even more tightly. At that moment, a dark shadow and cold breeze overwhelmed her. She turned around anxiously when she saw a man, about 5 ft 9 wearing a mask. He swiftly put a black bag over her head, snatched her phone out of her hand and threw it into the bushes. Mimi began to scream and tried to fight her way out of it.

"Shut up, or I will shoot you," the man whispered in her ear. He picked her up with great strength, dumped her into the boot of a car, and drove off, leaving her phone and car with their trackers in the car park.

Mimi's heart was pounding in the back of the boot. She came to the stark realisation that she had been kidnapped. Mimi wondered how anybody was going to find her when she had no clue where she was, and she had become separated from both bugging devices.

After a reasonably short drive, the car suddenly stopped. Soon, Mimi could hear footsteps crunching gravel, approaching the boot where she was. She thought about running and escaping once the boot was opened - but in the midst of her fears, she realised she could not risk it. She had two boys to raise, and death was not an option. She began to say a prayer.

"Dear Lord, you know where I am, you know who has taken me. I pray holy spirit that you will send your angels to protect me and find me to bring me back to my family. In Jesus' name."

Suddenly Mimi remembered one of Kika's 'Cards of Courage'.

"But Jesus spoke to them at once. "Don't be afraid", he said. "Take courage! I am here!" Mark 6:50.

Mimi chanted the scripture under her breath and believed every word of it. She believed that God was with her, and she did not need to be afraid.

Suddenly the boot of the car opened, and the man lifted her and took her into a dark room. He sat her down on the floor and tied up her hands and her feet. He then proceeded to take the bag off her face.

When Mimi saw the person, her heart sank. Rayo was looking straight at her, holding a gun to her head.

Kika

Kika had raced out to Mrs Coker's house, panicking. She hoped Dami and the police officers had located Mimi, and she was safe. Or she was at the meeting, and Dami just got the wrong information about who she was with.

As she got there, Mimi's home was like a circus. There were multiple police officers, red and blue lights flashing, and Mimi's mother was weeping. Kika gulped. "This does not look good," she thought to herself.

She saw Dami on the phone in the corner of the living room and walked up to him.

"Dami," she screamed while hugging him, "what is going on - have we found Mimi?"

Dami shook his head, "We tracked the car and phone down to this deserted hotel. Her phone was smashed in a bush, and the car was abandoned; we even went into the hotel. I think it is clear that Mimi has been abducted, and my guess is Rayo has taken her." Dami said apprehensively.

He was trying to keep calm, but you could tell he was petrified. "So, we currently have a search party out looking for her."

Kika looked at Dami in dismay. She had always thought that if a kidnapper wanted to abduct someone, the first thing they would do to avoid being caught would be to destroy the person's phone and car.

She shook her head.

"Come with me," she pulled Dami's hand and rushed to find Mimi's mum.

Mimi

"You went online to speak poorly of me, you turn the world against me, and you try to set me up with the police - you think I don't know about the car and the phone," Rayo laughed evilly to himself.

Mimi looked straight at him. At this point, she felt that this was the end - this was how she was going to die. Rayo was angry, and he seemed drunk. Which meant he was capable of doing anything. She also knew there seemed no chance of her being found by anyone. However, although she was petrified, she strangely felt in control.

"Rayo, how could you do that to us. How could you put your wife and kids in jeopardy like that? Do you know how many people wanted to harass and kill me?" She said boldly.

Rayo looked over at Mimi in disbelief. "Did you not receive my letter?" He said in anger, "I told you I did it for you guys. Can I control how others will react? I have invested all that money abroad, and it will generate huge returns to cater to all of us, long into the future."

"Rayo, so where have you been these last few months?" Mimi asked. She realised that she might be able to talk

Rayo out from potentially shooting her. He seemed like he was willing to explain himself.

"I have been in Australia, and I have been keeping a watchful eye over you from there," he said.

"In what way?" Mimi was freaked out by Rayo's stalking antics.

"Social media - and when I saw that video of you, Mimi, I was mad and angry. But I love you so much, and because of this, I have a proposition for you," Rayo continued. "Lets go away to Australia with the boys, and no one ever needs to find us again."

Mimi looked at Rayo from head to toe. She could not believe in any way Rayo would think she wanted to restart any form of relationship with him, especially after kidnapping her and pointing a gun at her head. But Mimi was a woman of wisdom. She knew if she did not play along, Rayo would probably kill her instantly without a second thought. So she did.

"So what is the plan?" Mimi asked.

"Well, you need to go home and tell everyone you are fine, and that the meeting with the governor went well. In the middle of the night, I will meet you outside your mother's house in a rented car, you will bring the boys out into the car, and we will all make our way to Australia to live a completely new life. There is a ship that would take us to London, and we can catch a flight from there. I have already organised passports and disguises." He offered.

"Okay, that sounds like a pretty straightforward plan. I am down!" Mimi thought there would easily be ways to figure out an escape plan if Rayo allows her to leave.

"Oh, and don't even think about setting me up or I will kill you and your whole family," he said while waving the gun. "Including the boys," he began to snigger.

Mimi gulped.

Kika

"Mrs Coker, Mrs Coker!" Kika screamed as she finally found her in the boy's bedroom.

"Yes, dear?" She said, still sniffling and trying not to think that she may not see her daughter again.

"Sorry to disturb you, ma, but do you know whether Mimi wore some new diamond earrings today when she was going out?"

Mrs Coker looked at Kika disappointedly.

"I don't think this is the time Kika," Dami said, reading Mrs Coker's face.

"Trust me," she said to him. "Mrs Coker, do you remember?"

Mrs Coker thought about it, "yes, she showed me the new diamond earrings you gave to her, and she was wearing them when she was leaving."

Kika smiled. "Great, there's a tracker in the earrings!"

Mrs Coker screamed, "Oh, so where is she then?"

"I need your wifi to check. I'm out of data. I wanted to make sure she had the earrings before I asked you for the wifi passcode," Kika explained.

Dami looked at Kika in disbelief and admiration. He could not believe she had gone out of her way to put a tracker in earrings and not tell anyone.

Mrs Coker quickly gave Kika the password. As they checked, they found that Mimi was in an isolated building in Lekki. Not too far from where they were.

"Let's go, go, go!" Dami screamed at the police officers. "Mrs Coker, please stay here and pray for us, we are going to bring her back."

Mrs Coker nodded.

"Kika, we need your app, I have a dongle. Oh, and I need you for moral support," he said, smiling. He bent his head down towards her to kiss her. Kika smiled and returned the kiss. They spent a few seconds gazing into each other's eyes.

"Okay, we need to go," she said to Dami.

Mimi

"So, can I trust you to do what you are told?" Rayo asked sternly.

Mimi nodded. She was so focused on getting out of that situation; she would say anything to keep Rayo calm.

""Wear this watch; it will track your goings and comings. If it comes off or is left somewhere else - I would know instantly that you are doing something out of line. It also monitors what you say," Rayo said, laughing evilly, "All the gadgets are from overseas."

A great feeling of defiance came across Mimi. Was it worth it? Was it worth living in any more fear? At this point, Mimi was ready to let this end; however it was going to. She knew God was in control of the situation. "Rayo, I can't!"

"You can't what?" Rayo asked.

"I cannot wear that watch, and I cannot promise that I would not seek help," Mimi said dismayed, but now fearless. She thought to herself that she would rather die than continue this charade and put her family in danger. "So please do as you please - kill me. Just know justice will be served."

Rayo looked at her in disbelief. He could not believe Mimi was willing to die than to spend the rest of her life with him. "Well, if I cannot be with you, no one else can - ," he pointed the gun back at Mimi. Mimi closed her eyes and tensed her body. "Oh, and just to let you know that after I kill you, I am going to kill those boys and your mother."

Mimi's eyes widened.

Rayo was about to pull the trigger when the door to the apartment swung open.

A gunshot went off.

Kika screamed.

Dami yelled.

Mimi cried.

But it was Rayo who had been shot dead in the head by the police officers, who had rushed in at the right time.

Mimi looked up and saw Dami and Kika running to her side.

She wept on Kika's shoulder, relieved to see her. Kika held her tightly and began to cry too. One second later, Mimi would have been the one lying dead on the floor. Dami wrapped his arms around both women.

"How did you find me?" she finally had the courage to say.

"Your friend Kika is some agent," he joked, still tense from the episode. "Those earrings she gave you, have trackers embedded in them," Dami said, smiling at Kika.

"What?!" Mimi said, touching her earrings.

"I just knew that nobody will ever suspect it. We had access to a lot of these monitoring devices at 'Hello Lagos' – and I asked my friend, Daisy to get me some, seeing as I no longer work there. We needed to keep you safe," Kika said, holding Mimi tightly.

"Wow, 'Hello Lagos' was good for something," Mimi said, relieved. She looked at Rayo's dead body on the ground. She could not believe she had escaped a monster, and he was gone forever.

"Thank you, Jesus!"

A journal to the reader

Dear Reader,

I am extremely happy for Mimi. Can you imagine going through a period where every day, there is an underlying fear of something negative happening?

I loved her attitude when she felt her life was about to be over. She knew she would be alright, and that Rayo would be caught either way. She knew that God was in control of the situation.

I am sure you can imagine how she must feel now that she is saved - elated, free, relieved. She did not want to die, but she held onto God and knew it was all going to work out for her good. (Romans 8:28).

God always comes through at the right time. He makes a way when there seems to be no way. I am sure there are many times you encounter ways God has come through for you. So, when you hit a bumpy road in your life, why be anxious?

I know it is easier said than done, I am talking to myself as well. There have been many times when I get worried about something, and I know I should pray, I know everything is going to be alright, yet I will be having panic attacks about it. Below is my favourite verse that helps me get through.

"Do not be anxious about anything, but in every situation, by prayer and petition, with thanksgiving, present your requests to God and the peace of God, which transcends all understanding, will guard your hearts and your minds in Christ Jesus." Philippians 4:6-7.

The scripture reminds me to be thankful. To praise God like my problem has already been solved. In fact, all I have to do is play some worship music on my phone, and I instantly become more relaxed.

Journal Task 13: Write out Psalm 100: 1-5 from the Bible. Whenever you are anxious about something, read this scripture out loud. You are praising his name for what he has already done.

Tip: Do not lose faith during tough times. Believe that God is in control over everything.

Lots of Love X

Simi Alexis Romeo

CHAPTER FOURTEEN
6 MONTHS LATER

Tara

"Aww, Dabira, she is adorable," Tara said, excitedly while she FaceTimed her new baby niece, Dunsin Edoh.

"She can't wait to meet you, Tara," Dabira said, placing Dunsin on her lap. "You look like you are on your way somewhere - Is that a 'Tara Cole Collection' outfit?" Dabira asked.

"I am on my way to a session with Pastor Lade and then off to Kika's launch. And yes, it is! It's a new one!" Tara giggled. "The brand has been getting a lot of positive reviews, and Bode is so proud of how well I did without his financial backing. Now that we have gotten our money back after the Australian police officers helped to recover it, he has invested millions of Naira into expanding the brand. We are currently in talks with organisers of 'New York Fashion Week', regarding getting featured this year!"

"What?!" Dabira gasped. "That is amazing news! Congratulations, Tara!"

"We haven't secured it yet, but thank you so much for all your support," Tara said graciously.

Dabira smiled, "So how is everything with you and the girls, have you spoken to Anita?"

Dabira had gone back to London after all the drama with Anita and Nati. She had sent a long letter apologising to Anita and hoped she would forgive her.

Anita did not respond.

"Well, Anita has assured me that she does not have a problem with me, but I do feel our friendship has become a bit strained, which is a shame," Tara said sadly. "Also, sometimes, I want to post my beautiful niece on social media to celebrate her, and I can't because I am aware of how Anita would feel."

"I am so sorry, Tara, for putting you in this position," Dabira said, still feeling terribly guilty. "Anita did not deserve this. She is literally the kindest person. The fact that she encouraged Nati to have a relationship with Dunsin shows her heart. I could not be more disgusted with myself."

"Dabira, honestly, you have beaten yourself up about this for long enough. I think you should learn from it and move on," Tara comforted.

"Yeah, I guess!" Dabira said.

For her, it was easier said than done. She knew she acted out of line and had to deal with the consequences of her actions for the rest of her life; the guilt, the shame, and the stigma of raising a child as a single mother.

However, she did feel Dunsin was the only positive thing that came out of the situation.

"Anyway, Dabira, I am about to enter the church build-ing. I will speak to you soon, especially about the wedding plans." Tara shrieked.

"Oh, exciting, I can't wait. Love you, sis." Dabira

brought Dunsin close to the camera, and Tara kissed her through the screen.

"Love you too."

"Tara, you are looking fabulous," Pastor Lade said, admiring her. "Tell me what has been going on?"

Tara could not stop smiling.

She was in a great place. The last year had definitely taken a toll on her, but she was happy because she knew if the tough times had not occurred, she would never have grown to be the woman she is today.

"Well, Bode and I are excited to start our wedding plans. We have set a date for March, next year."

"That is great news, Tara, how many people are you inviting?" Pastor Lade asked, making light of the fact that when she met Tara and Bode for a counselling session nearly a year ago, Tara was focused on inviting approximately one thousand people.

Tara laughed, "I have reduced the headcount to five hundred, I want it to be as intimate as it can be for a Nigerian wedding. It is not necessary to invite people and pay for them, especially when very few showed us any compassion when Bode and I were struggling financially."

"Exactly! Wow, you really have come a long way. Well done, Tara!" Pastor Lade said ecstatically. "Have you heard from your mother?"

"She still wants nothing to do with me, unfortunately. I still pray for her daily. Hopefully, one day she will open her heart to me and see me as a blessing," Tara said, looking to the ground and playing with her fingers.

"Tara, you are a blessing, and God will reward you for

your efforts. Keep staying close to his word and surround yourself with those that love you."

Tara smiled, "Thanks for this, Pastor Lade. I have to run to pick Bode. We are heading to my friend Kika's launch."

"Okay, dear! God bless."

Anita

"So if you just sign here, Ms Fawun, your divorce will be finalised," her divorce attorney expressed.

Anita picked up her pen and signed the documents. She was relieved that the process of divorce was finally over. She had barely spoken to Nati personally and did everything through her lawyers. He had tried to reach out to her several times, but Anita wanted nothing more to do with him.

The only time she felt a need to contact him was when Dabira had given birth. Tara expressed to her that Nati wanted nothing to do with Dabira or the baby. She pleaded with Anita to persuade him, as she knows how her own mother's rejection had affected her. Tara knew that Nati would do anything for Anita because of how much he wanted her back.

Anita was also aware that it was not the child's fault, so agreed to contact Nati through a letter expressing how it will be detrimental to the child, and he should hold himself accountable for his mistakes and do his best to learn from them.

Nati heeded the advice and quickly contacted Dabira, secretly hoping Anita would forgive him. However, Anita felt she needed to move on and focus on being the best version of herself. She noticed that even when she and Nati were good, she was unable to reach her full potential with him. If anything, she is grateful for what happened as her vision for where she wanted to reach and be, became a lot clearer.

"You are now a free bird, Ms Fawun," The lawyer said.

Anita smiled - she did feel free.

"Hey, mummy," Anita called as she entered her three-bedroom penthouse apartment in Banana Island, Ikoyi.

"Anita!" Aisha Fawun screamed as she hugged her daughter, "How did it go?"

"Well, we are divorced now," Anita said, shrugging. Although she knew she did not want a life with Nati any longer, she was still sad that it had to end in such a hurtful way. She hoped that she would eventually be able to forgive him entirely. She wanted to, but it was hard."

"Well, I do have some good news," Aisha said, smiling.

"Oh, I need some good news mummy, what is it?" Anita responded in anticipation.

"Nati has just formally resigned from Fawun Investment Ltd," Aisha continued.

Anita's eyes widened, "What?"

"I know, it took a while, and we had to give him a huge payoff, but if your father were alive and knew all that he had put you through, he would have fired him immediately. All we did was advise him to resign amicably. When he signed the divorce papers, he probably knew he had to."

Anita felt that Nati should leave their family business, especially when he was not going to be part of the family any longer. Nati put up a fight about it, but it seems like her mother speaking to him and pushing him to resign was the best thing.

"Wow, thank you, mummy, for all your support, it has been really nice having you around."

Aisha laughed, "That day you kicked me out of Kika's flat, made me think and look at myself."

Anita smiled awkwardly, "sorry about that."

"No, don't be sorry - you were right. You need to value yourself and not allow people to disrespect you. Even if it is your husband or mother," she said, winking mischievously. "Especially when you have been nothing but a good person to them. I wish I knew this during my marriage. It would have made me a better, stronger person."

"Aww, mum, you did the best you could," Anita said, rubbing her mother's back.

"I need to start getting ready for Kika's launch event, where is Caleb?"

A month prior, Anita had decided to adopt Caleb. She had been attending church religiously and became very close to Madame Pat, the orphanage's house-mother. She told Anita that she had a nurturing spirit and soul and that since she had developed this strong connection to Caleb, why didn't she adopt him.

Anita had always been open to adoption even when she was married to Nati, but he was so against it, so they never did. She prayed about it and concluded that adopting Caleb was most likely part of her purpose.

"He is upstairs sleeping," Aisha responded.

"Thank you for being the best grandmother to him, mummy," Anita said, tearing up, "Are you happy to babysit him while I attend Kika's launch?"

"Absolutely."

Mimi

"So Mimi, six months ago, you were tied up in an uncompleted building in Lekki, with a gun being pointed at your head, and now you are a best-selling author. How did you get from there to this point?" Roma from 'The Roma Show' asked.

Mimi sighed as she remembered the events that brought her to the point of releasing her first book, 'Blinded by Abuse'.

"Roma, the whole experience with my late husband, had been a significant journey, and I learnt so much about myself. I wish I got to know my husband a lot longer and better before we got married, but guess what, I didn't." Mimi said smugly, "that fateful day at the Award show when he threw a tantrum because he did not win an award, that should have been a red flag. He is entitled to be upset and disappointed - absolutely. But did he need to storm out and make a scene?"

Mimi continued to recall her relationship with Rayo. She spoke about how she did not listen to those who knew her and had her best interest at heart. She spoke about the verbal abuse that quickly turned physical and how it began to hurt her business and relationships.

"Roma, although it has been tough, I am grateful for the experience, and most importantly, for my two greatest gifts, Desmond and Daniel. I wrote this book 'Blinded by Abuse' because I wish to help other women who may be going through the same thing. As women, we know when something is not right, but we are so compassionate and forgiving that we let it go. We need to be bold and say enough is enough!"

"Absolutely! Well, thank you, Mimi, for coming onto the show this morning. To get the book 'Blinded by Abuse' by Mimi Coker, please visit our website, which is now visible on the screen."

"It's a wrap!" One of the cameramen called out.

Mimi got up from her chair to thank Roma and the crew.

"Mimi, your story is so inspiring. Thank you for writing this and helping others. It is going to go a long way." Roma continued.

"Thank you, Roma; by God's grace," they hugged, and Mimi left the set.

Mimi's life had all of a sudden become very busy. Writing a book on her struggles with Rayo was hot news, and every media house in Nigeria was desperate for an interview with her. What made Mimi laugh was how 'Hello Lagos' would not stop pestering her too. But after all they did to her, and to Kika, she knew she would never waste her breath on them.

Business had picked up heavily as well. In fact, after 'The Roma Show', Mimi had to head to Kika's launch event. She was not just going there as a guest, but Kika had hired her to plan it. Mimi was so proud of Kika and was more than happy to be a part of the next journey in her life.

As soon as she got backstage, Mrs Coker was waiting with Daniel and Desmond, who were jumping up and down happily. Mimi was so grateful for her mother - she had dedicated her life to taking care of her and her sons.

"I love you, boys," Mimi said while carrying both children, one in each arm. "Do you love mummy?" She asked them.

"Daniel, Desmond, give mummy a kiss!" Mrs Coker said.

Both boys leant towards Mimi and kissed her on the cheek.

Mimi's heart was full.

Kika

"Can we please give it up for Kika Taiwo on the launch of the 'My Potential is Limitless' blog," the MC called out.

About 150 people stood up to applaud Kika as she made her way to the stage. She looked around, admiring all the people there that had believed in her. She looked at her close friends Mimi, Tara, Anita, who could not stop screaming, "We love you, Kika!". Her boyfriend, Dami Dare, smiled proudly and gave her a wink when they caught each other's eye. Her friends, Ola and Daisy, were also in the crowd sitting right next to her parents, who had flown in from Abuja to be there. She was overwhelmed with joy.

It had been a long six months since Kika had unfairly been let go from her 'dream' job at 'Hello Lagos'. Her friends had regularly advised her to start a blog about female empowerment. They saw something in Kika that she was unable to see in herself.

"I want to thank everyone for coming to the 'My Potential is Limitless' blog launch." She said, addressing the crowd. "My journey up until this point has been a rollercoaster. In my teenage years, I was incredibly insecure and showed myself no love. I went through a period of discovering myself and how God sees me. It made me a better person, and I am grateful." Kika smiled, remembering how argumentative she was and how much she felt undervalued.

"Then once I got through that hurdle, well, at least I thought I did."

The crowd tittered.

"I began working at where I believed was my dream

job - one of the top media houses in Nigeria. I was ecstatic and thought I had made it. However, I was there for eight years and had nothing to show for it. I valued that job more than I valued myself. I put that job before everything, even before God sometimes." Kika reminisced about how that job will affect her dating life, Christian life, and her friends' and family's lives.

She began to tear up.

"I lowered my standards, and it was only when it got to a point where they were trying to change my character that I had to stand firm and tell them 'No'. That resulted in me being fired."

Kika took a long pause.

"So why am I telling you this? Like I said, life is a rollercoaster - it is up and down. When I was going through my struggles with insecurity, I was down; I overcame it, I was up. I worked at a place that did not see my worth; I was down and, now I am starting a blog; I am up. This does not mean it would never go down again, but I know from experience that I will go up from any down situation."

She sighed.

"So, what is my constant?" Kika said, rhetorically asking the crowd. "It is God. His love has been my constant, His friendship, His mercies, His goodness. Which is why in the good times and the bad times, we should always rely on God. He knows us better than we know ourselves."

The crowd all stood up to applaud Kika. She laughed awkwardly because she had not finished.

"So now, going into why I started this blog. Everyone has been created for one reason, and one reason only - that is to glorify God and grow His kingdom. But everyone has their own path to travel towards achieving this, and every individual has various multiple ways to achieve this. It could be your career, your talents, your personality traits, your experiences."

She paused again.

"I am Kika Taiwo; I am a writer, I am Nigerian, I am a Christian, I love to journal, to design, and I am all about female empowerment. My friends describe me as fun and crazy, I went through a period of insecurity, a hard time at work, and now I have started this blog and have a stationery brand. God is my architect. He designed me and made me this way. Each thing he put in me will be used to glorify his name - none of it is by accident. The funny thing is as I encounter new experiences, more will be added to my life to help fulfil my purpose. My potential is limitless."

Kika looked at her friend's in the crowd. "I want to invite my best friends up here to speak and share their stories. Please can we put our hands together for Mimi, Tara, and Anita!"

The ladies made their way to the stage and began to introduce themselves.

"I am Mimi Coker; I am the mother of beautiful twin baby boys. I am an event planner and author. I recently just became a widow. I went through a scary period in my life where I was being abused physically, mentally, and emotionally. I am thankful that I came through that period in my life. My potential is limitless!"

The crowd applauded Mimi.

"I am Tara Williams; I am a blessing from a negative situation. I used to dwell on it and tell people I was a product of rape, but now I say I am a blessing from it. I am engaged and soon to be Mrs Tara Cole; I have a fashion label - The Tara Cole Collection. All my life, I have felt abandoned and neglected and would lash out at those close to me. I am blessed to have amazing friends and family who never neglected or abandoned me during this time. My husband-to-be and I have just come out of a tough financial situation, and it has made me a stronger and wiser woman. My potential is limitless!"

The crowd applauded Tara. Kika was proud of how far Tara had come with her struggles.

"I am Anita Fawun. First, I would like to say how I am a strong, independent woman!"

The crowd all screamed and clapped their hands. Anita laughed before eventually clearing her throat.

"I have found a close relationship with God and have learnt to rely on him. A year ago, I went through a tough period in my life where I had a miscarriage and lost my husband on the same day. It was hard for me because my marriage was my identity, and I depended on my husband for everything. I was at the lowest of the lows. I was married for eight years and was unable to have children. My marriage ended due to infidelity and a breakdown of trust. Now I can stand firm and reach for my full potential. I am now a new mum. A month ago, I adopted my son, Caleb. My divorce was finalised this morning, and I am excited about the future - for what God has in store for me. My potential is limitless."

The crowd went wild, screaming, clapping. Kika looked over at Tara, who was leading the screams. The Tara of a year ago would have had a different reaction.

"Wow, these are my friends, guys! I could not be more proud. Is there anybody in the audience who would like to introduce themselves and tell their story?" Kika asked.

"I would!" A loud, bold voice came from the back of the room.

Kika gasped. The woman made her way to the stage in a long flowing maxi dress and a turban. All four ladies gulped, and Kika slowly gave her the microphone, nervous for what she would say.

"Hi everybody, I am Ms Chigozie Antoinette Nkiru, also know as Ms Gozy, and I am a broken woman. I am divorced, my children cannot stand me, I have no friends, and I have hurt so many people due to our debased journalism at 'Hello Lagos'. Nine years ago, I hired this incredibly smart, well-spoken, and passionate individual, Kika Taiwo. She was so inspirational and reminded me of myself. I demanded, and took so much from her and did not give her any credit for it. I was fearful she would grow and take away the only thing that had ever been of value to me, my job. I refused to promote her, but I did not want her to leave. I fired her as a bluff, hoping she would come begging for her job back, and I would have hired her back instantly at the same level and kept her there suppressed."

She paused…

"Ever since Kika left 'Hello Lagos', our ratings have plunged, she had become core to my effectiveness in running the business, and I had come to rely on her for the creative side as well. She wrote impeccable stories that I took credit for, for which I am now ashamed. Three months ago, I decided to step down as editor-in-chief and become a board member solely. I took this time to work on myself, and I found God in the process."

She turned to look at Kika.

"Kika, I want to tell you that I am sorry, I think you are incredible, and I am proud of how far you have come. This was all you, as I had nothing to do with where you are today. It shows that if God is for you, none can be against you. To show my support, I would like to donate N25 million to your blog, with no strings attached. This is an accumulation of all the promotion money and commission you should have received as earnings from 'Hello Lagos' over the years."

Kika was in shock by Ms Gozy's speech and the amount of money she was giving to her. She went over to Ms Gozy and hugged her. "I forgave you a long time ago, Ms Gozy. Thank you so much."

Ms Gozy began to tear up, "Mimi Coker, I apologise for all the pain 'Hello Lagos' caused you too, and anyone else here we have hurt with our stories. I am sorry. As I am a board member for 'Hello Lagos', I will be working to change our narrative. We no longer will publish lies and untruths, and embellish stories about individuals, but will exalt women encourage self-awareness and development, and promote the 'My Potential is Limitless' blog. And we will pay Kika Taiwo a fee of N2 million a month for it to be featured in our publications. Kika, it is time for 'Hello Lagos' to celebrate you."

The crowd erupted in cheers and applause as Ms Gozy handed Kika a cheque. "She hurried off the stage and left the hall. She hoped she had been able to show to Kika that she only had positive intentions for her, but more importantly, that she had assuaged the guilt of her bad behaviour of the past.

"Kika, this event is amazing! Imagine that Ms Gozy sees your value now," Tara said to Kika as all four girls were sitting down, sipping their cocktails.

"Honestly, I am still in shock!" Kika responded.

"Girls, now that everybody's lives are somewhat back to normal, we need to start doing brunch on Sundays again," Anita added. "I want to know how everyone is doing and coping," she looked at Tara, "believe it or not, I want to hear about your new niece, my sort of ex-stepdaughter," she said, making light of the situation.

The girls laughed awkwardly.

"And now that Tara has secured a date for her wedding, and Kika is pretty much going to marry my lawyer," Mimi added jovially, "I have two weddings to plan!" She laughed.

"Let's not get ahead of ourselves," Kika giggled. "Dami and I have been together for six months. I am excited for you and Anita to start dating these Lagos boys."

Mimi and Tara fell over each other laughing, but Anita was distracted.

"Anita, are you okay?" Kika asked.

Anita stared at her phone, "erm yeah," she sighed, "I have just received a message from Nati," she looked up at the girls with pain in her eyes, "his mother just died."

A journal to the reader

Dear Reader,

Sorry to leave you on a cliff hanger. I did not think it was realistic to round up everything in their lives because it does not end there. The journey of life continues. Though it all seems like everything has been concluded in this chapter of the ladies' lives, God has a lot more in store for them. A lot more situations where they will laugh, cry, and will have to bounce back from.

The same goes for you.

Your life is ongoing until your last day on earth. And for believers, we know there is life after death, so it never ends.

This is to encourage you that there is so much more you are going to achieve.

When God gave me the idea to write this book, it was funny because I don't like to read. If I had to read something, it would have to be juicy. Hence why stories in the Bible appeal to me more. So, I thought creating a fiction novel would be more down my alley.

This is May 2020, and 7 months ago, if you told me I would be writing a novel, I would have literally laughed out loud.

The thing that blows my mind is that God always knew.

I reminisce about situations that came naturally to me. For instance, when I was four years old, I wrote my own collection of books. Each book entailed 2 A4 sheets of paper folded in half and stapled at the fold. I had about 12 of them and left them at an activity centre (it still pains me till this day that I don't have them)

I also remember how I used to get into trouble in school for daydreaming and going into a 'trance'. In my head, I would imagine scenarios and situations. There definitely is a time and a place, but those were signs that showed writing a fictional story has always been part of my purpose. I am excited about what else God has planned for my life.

Now, what about you?

Journal Task 14: In journal 11, you wrote down a list of everything you are believing God for. Now I would like you to create a vision board of this.

You can do this digitally or physically.

Collect images and words of things you hope to achieve in the future. Stick it on a board and place it somewhere that you know you will see it daily. This is to remind you of your vision and allow you not to lose hope.

Tip: Habakuk 2:2 "And the LORD answered me: "Write the vision; make it plain on tablets, so he may run who reads it."

P.s I hope you enjoyed the book, here's to next time.

Lots of Love X

Simi Alexis Romeo

I know that you can do all things; no purpose of yours can be thwarted.

Job 42:2

About the Author

Simi Alexis Romeo was brought up both in London, UK, and Lagos, Nigeria. She has a First-Class degree in Architectural Design and Technology from Coventry University, UK, and a Masters' in Interior Design from Florence, Italy. She currently works as an Interior Designer in London.

She has a passion for helping women struggling with low self-esteem as she understands the implications it can have on their lives from her own experiences, both personal and observed. She desires for these women to realise their worth, appreciate their strengths, and fulfil their God-given purpose. She volunteers as a mentor in the Esther's Mentoring Scheme programme in Jesus House, UK.

Simi founded a Children's Charity in 2015 in Lagos, Nigeria, called Happy Kids - Promising Purpose, whose mission is to give orphans and underprivileged children a sense of hope and future.

In her spare time, she loves to practice yoga, experience new restaurants, and generally find inspiration on what life has to offer, in those little things God has blessed the world with.

She believes God has so much more in store for her as she continues on her journey of discovering her specific purpose.

CONNECT WITH ME

@_simialexis
@ajournaltoyou
www.ajournaltoyou.com
info@ajournaltoyou.com

Lightning Source UK Ltd.
Milton Keynes UK
UKHW011619121020
371441UK00002B/445